Two Cases of Institutionalizing Service Learning:

How Campus Climate Affects the Change Process

*Including the
History, Context and
Development of Campus
Compact's Project on Integrating
Service with Academic Study*

Marie Troppe, *editor*

The Project on Integrating Service with Academic Study (SAS) provides training, advice on strategy and technical assistance to colleges and universities that are working to build community service into their teaching and research. While it provides some resources for individual faculty (such as a database of courses and syllabi), the project works primarily with campuses attempting to institutionalize service-based teaching and research. Campuses are typically motivated to integrate service into teaching and research by some mixture of concerns regarding citizenship, diversity or building community. Much of the project's actual work focuses on integrating service with the curriculum, because we recognize that the curriculum is the core institutional structure around which most campuses are organized. The Project has been funded by the Ford Foundation and an anonymous donor.

Project on Integrating Service with Academic Study Staff:
Sandra Enos, Project Director
Marie Troppe, Project Associate
Kate Jackson, Project Intern

Campus Compact: The Project for Public and Community Service is a coalition of over 500 college and university presidents who believe that institutions of higher education hold a primary responsibility to foster students' sense of civic responsibility and to contribute to the welfare of their communities. The Compact works on a national level to cultivate discourse and support for issues of public service; develop resource materials, grant programs, workshops and institute; and support a network of state and specialized offices to provide targeted programs for campuses. Campus Compact, Box 1975, Brown University, Providence, RI 02912-1975, (401) 863-1119.

Campus Compact is a project of the Education Commission of the States, a non-profit, nationwide interstate compact formed in 1965. The primary purpose of the Commission is to help governors, state legislators, state education officials and others develop policies to improve the quality of education at all levels. It is the policy of the Education Commission of the States to take affirmative action to prevent discrimination in its policies, programs and employment practices. Education Commission of the States, 707 17th Street, Suite 2700, Denver, CO 80202-3427, (303) 299-3600.

Copies of this book are available for $10.00 from Campus Compact, Box 1975, Brown University, Providence, RI 02912. Phone (401)863-1119, email *campus@compact.org*.

Acknowledgements

Campus Compact thanks those who contributed their thoughts and writings: Patricia Bacon, Avonnee Brown, Kristen Ann Cotter, Dave Crowner, Brian Harward, Kristine Hughey, Tim Leary, Karl Mattson, Ilona McGuinness, Keith Morton, Ralph Sorensen, Erin Swezey, Dora Townsend and Stacey Zeller.

We extend special thanks to Kate Jackson, our student intern. Without her support this publication would not have been possible.

The Morton/Troppe article was first published in Volume 15, No. 1 of the Journal of Business Ethics, January 1996. It is reprinted with permission from Kluwer Academic Publishers.

The Compact gratefully acknowledges the Ford Foundation and an anonymous donor for support of the Project on Integrating Service with Academic Study.

Table of Contents

Foreword

For many years, student enthusiasm and community need have made community service a popular activity on college campuses throughout the nation. Service learning, the academic counterpart to traditional community service, has grown increasingly in the last five years. Service learning, however, faces more institutional challenges than does traditional community service. Faculty sometimes wrongly assume that service learning awards academic credit for hours of service and not for learning; thus they perceive it as a threat to academic rigor and oppose it at every opportunity. Those faculty, however, who are willing to consider service learning as a new pedagogy might not have the knowledge of how to apply service learning methods within their discipline nor do they feel rewarded by review and tenure committees for doing so. Student affairs professionals who have typically run numerous community service and service learning programs, may not necessarily have much experience understanding the motivations and modus operandi of faculty. With these limitations being brought to the table, faculty and administrators often find it difficult to support new service learning courses as they are implemented on various campuses.

The Morton/Troppe article introduces the two case studies by way of delineating the history, context and development of Campus Compact's Project on Integrating Service with Academic Study. By 1990, Campus Compact, which was founded in 1985, recognized that in order for service to become an integral part of higher education, it had to be tied to the academic mission of the campus. Responding to this realization, Campus Compact launched the Project on Integrating Service with Academic Study and its Summer Institute in 1991. In three years, teams from over 60 campuses attended the Institutes, developed

action plans for their campuses, and participated in follow-up workshops, implementation grants, phone interviews, surveys and site visits. In 1994, the Project began hosting seven Regional Institutes each year that expanded the reach of the original Summer Institutes.

The Project does not endorse a single model of the institutionalization of service learning. Indeed, every campus must scrutinize its own strengths, weaknesses, opportunities, threats, cultures and climates and find an organic model that can take root in its unique environment. Teams attending the Institutes from 1991 to 1993 found that they could learn from their similarities and differences. Institutional type became an important variable; small, liberal arts colleges, for example, found that they could try strategies that had worked at other similar institutions. Religiously-affiliated colleges whose service was based in matters of faith discovered that public institutions, whose service was based in ideals of citizenship, could nonetheless offer experience in connecting service learning to the mission of a campus.

The following case studies by no means prescribe a formula that will ensure successful institutionalization efforts. With the benefit of hindsight, they outline the process of institutionalization as it occurred over three years or more. Some of the events and milestones they describe seem artificially easy to achieve when put into this overall context. But, at the time these events occurred they were often accompanied by intense discussion, power struggles and lack of shared vision about future directions.

The two colleges featured in this publication, Loyola College and Gettysburg College, have long histories of involving their students in service to the community. They were chosen for several reasons. These schools had established community service centers prior to the surge of campuses who began to create their centers in response to the Corporation for National Service funding. These two schools are small in size and thus it was slightly easier to describe the institutionalization process for them than for larger schools. Other practitioners in the service learning field considered Loyola and Gettysburg's service learning programs successful. Site visits required by a Campus Compact grant were a convenient starting point. And, finally, it seemed more useful to compare two schools of similar institutional types than two schools in completely different sectors.

Gettysburg and Loyola are similar in that they both have a religious foundation, the former Lutheran and the latter Jesuit (Catholic). Undergraduate teaching is valued at these small, liberal arts colleges. Although Loyola serves an urban community and Gettysburg a rural one, their service learning programs both grew out of roots in their campus ministry departments. Gettysburg established its Center for Public Service in 1991 and Loyola established its Center for Values and Service in 1992. These Centers have enjoyed continuity of leadership. Both schools embrace a variety of curricular service learning options, for example, immersion trips, fourth credit option and full service learning courses.

What prompted service learning efforts before each school attended the Compacts's 1992 Summer Institute on Integrating Service with Academic Study? For Loyola, its 1989 accreditation self-study, its subsequent strategic planning and revision of the campus mission were initial motivations. These factors, coupled with a high level of student voluntarism, led its college council to approve a fourth credit option program in 1990 and to pilot service learning courses in 1991. In 1992 the president appointed a

committee of faculty, administration, students and community representatives to explore the integration of service with academic study. The rest unfolded from these origins.

In the case of Gettysburg, a 1979-1984 "January term" service learning program that included worldwide trips was the first antecedent for the culture of service that exists on the campus today. Other sparks for service learning initiatives included a well-placed bequest, a high level of student voluntarism within programs established since 1986, sociology service learning courses and chapel awareness trips to U.S. cities. And, in a manner similar to Loyola, Gettysburg's president appointed a Task Force on Servant Leadership in 1990 which further explored the opportunities of service learning. These factors converged and created a remarkable momentum for service.

Only in the last five years have Loyola and Gettysburg created, staffed and funded centers for service and launched conscious efforts to institutionalize service learning. In 1992, they both sent teams of faculty and administrators to the Summer Institute on Integrating Service with Academic Study sponsored by Campus Compact. After facing many obstacles, surprises and opportunities, they have both developed successful institutionalization strategies (explored here) that have given service learning a central place on their campuses. Their service learning programs and courses are continually evolving.

From the Margin to the Mainstream:
Campus Compact's Project on Integrating Service with Academic Study

Keith Morton and Marie Troppe

Abstract

This article offers an introduction to service learning and a brief review of the research on the effects of service learning on academic and values development. It outlines in detail the history of Campus Compact, an organization of 517 college and university presidents, and its Project on Integrating Service with Academic Study, along with lessons learned about institutionalizing service learning and information about resources for doing so. The findings are based on a three-year, national project supported by the Ford Foundation and an anonymous donor.

Service-Learning

Service learning is a form of experiential education, deeply rooted in cognitive and developmental psychology, pragmatic philosophy and democratic theory. It shares a common intellectual history with organizational development and participatory action research. Service learning is rooted, as well, in the formal and informal systems humans have developed to care for one another over time, ranging from individual spiritual practices such as charity, to voluntary associations meeting community needs, to human services institutions and welfare systems.

This is all by way of saying that service learning has no singular or simple definition, and that it is informed by a range of intellectual traditions and values systems, many of which seem to contradict or compete with one another. Sociologists using service learning as a vehicle to reinforce lessons about the relationship between personal income and quality of health care, for example, might find that they have little in common with philosophers who use service learning to teach about the meaning and limits of "charity." Or, these two teachers might find that they share a common framework of distributive justice and have independently selected a chapter on membership, community and distribution of social wealth from Michael Walzer's *Spheres of Justice*.

While no singular definition can be offered, it can be helpful to approach service learning as a pedagogy that works from a set of common assumptions about how people learn. David Kolb, in his groundbreaking study *Experiential Learning: Experience as the Source of Learning and Development*, argues that "Learning is the process whereby knowledge is created through the transformation of experience" (Kolb, 1984: 38). More to the point for business faculty, Kolb traces the shared lineage of experiential education and organizational development. Both emphasize subjective experience. For Kolb, the values of inquiry, choice and authenticity linked experiential education, organizational development and modern participative management philosophies.

In short, service learning theory begins with the assumption that experience is the foundation for learning; and various forms of community service are employed as the experiential basis for learning. These ideas are not new, and can be traced back at least to John Dewey and Jane Addams, who advocated for similar ideas beginning in the 1890s. Dewey recognized that people often learn best in teams, when they build upon what they already know, when they understand the purpose of what they are learning, when what they are learning clarifies their values, and through experimentation. In *Democracy and Education*, Dewey (1941) argued as well that education was the engine of democracy, and that locally based democracy was a political, cultural and social environment in which both individual and community could flourish.

Addams, in her turn, helped to transform the basic assumptions underlying the delivery of human services. What made her work revolutionary was the linking of two practices: systematically surveying the neighborhood surrounding Hull House (Addams' settlement house in Chicago) and insisting that, in the words of biographer Ellen Lagemann, "It was not for her to choose what services Hull House would offer. Hull House had to be ready to meet whatever needs its neighbors presented" (Lagemann, 1985: 25). The surveys were conducted jointly with social science faculty of the University of Chicago. Addams demonstrated the potential of working from an empirical, rather than a moral, definition of societal problems (Addams, 1910). In addition, Addams engaged current and recently graduated college students in service to the communities around her settlement houses.

Research Findings

Three recent studies suggest that service learning is an effective pedagogy for teaching both course content (academic concepts) and values. Markus, Howard and King (1993) conducted a comparative course section study of a large undergraduate political science course at the University of Michigan. They compared students in service learning sections of the course to students in the more traditional discussion sections of the course. The results suggest that service learning can

enhance students' intellectual development. In addition to having an effect on their personal values and orientations toward their community, the researchers "also found that students' academic learning was significantly enhanced by participation in course-relevant community service." (Markus, Howard and King, 1993: 416)

The larger implications of their research are an insistence that community service is important in higher education because of its educational benefits and a critique of traditional "top-down" approaches to learning or an "information-assimilation model." In such a model, students learn through abstraction rather than through direct experience. The information-assimilation model can transmit large volumes of information quickly and coherently but doesn't prove especially useful in helping students with long-term retention of information.

Service learning, in contrast, embraces learning as a "bottom-up" method, in which inductive reasoning is used to formulate general principles from direct personal experience. This approach is not known for its efficiency in transmitting large blocks of information, but it counters the abstractness of much classroom instruction. By engaging the student in real life situations, it motivates lasting learning.

In what is perhaps the most important point in their article, Markus and his colleagues conclude that educational institutions will value community service to the extent that it directly benefits students academically. They advocate for the integration of service learning with traditional classroom instruction. Markus, Howard and King (1993: 417) assert, "The kinds of service activities in which students participate should be selected so that they will illustrate, affirm, extend and challenge material presented in readings and lectures." Reflection and discussion must be a part of class meetings.

A second comparative course section study was done with a large undergraduate mass communication and society course at a research university, also with positive implications for service learning. Cohen and Kinsey (1994) reported that students and teaching assistants found experiential learning to enhance traditional teaching. They concluded: "Community service tied directly to academics — service learning — carries the promise of success in its potential to transport the student beyond the limiting cultural bounds of the text/lecture forms of the campus and outward into the larger social context from which, and for which, we construct the institutions of education" (Cohen and Kinsey, 1994: 13).

In a third study, Boss (1994) compared students in two sections of an undergraduate ethics course. The only significant difference in the way the sections were taught was community service. Boss assessed both the content learning of the students, and then, with assistance from a developmental psychologist, used James Rest's Defining Issues Test to measure gains in moral reasoning. She found that the group of students engaged in community service had a slightly better grasp of the course content and made significantly greater gains in moral reasoning than their counterparts in the non-service section. "This supports," writes Boss, "the claims of Kohlberg (1971) and Dewey (1939), as well as Gardner (1991), regarding the importance for moral development of real-life experience in confronting actual moral dilemmas" (Boss, 1994: 191).

If, as Markus, Cohen and Boss argue, service learning has the potential to be an effective pedagogy for both intellectual and moral development, why is it relatively uncommon on college campuses? Educators such as Jane Addams and John Dewey advocated for experiential, community-based learning as early as 1900. In the 1960's and 1970's, responding to the dramatic increase in urban violence, educators again sought to link service and higher education. Current national service programs gathered under the Corporation for National Service were prefigured in the University Year for Action, a federally funded program which involved 100 colleges and 10,000 college students in community service between 1971 and 1979.

Service learning is relatively uncommon, we argue, because of the general absence of institutional commitment to service learning by colleges and universities. Service learning is a relationship- and time-intensive pedagogy for both students and faculty. A sociology professor, in a recent interview, commented that his service learning course was "a peak teaching and learning experience for me and the students that had some positive impact on the community. But, he continued, "I don't know if I'll do it again soon." He was hesitant, he said, because service learning took more time than other forms of teaching and it was time away from his personal research and publishing. He felt forced to choose between service learning and formal advancement in his discipline. A meaningful goal in institutionalizing service learning on a college campus is supporting faculty so that they do not feel forced into such Hobbesian choices.

History of Campus Compact

The genesis and experience of Campus Compact and its Project on Integrating Service with Academic Study suggests some of what it means to institutionalize service learning on a college campus. Founded in 1985 with a membership of 23, Campus

Compact is now an organization of 517 college and university presidents committed to supporting community service on their campuses (see Table 1). In addition, Campus Compact has 18 state offices a network for historically black colleges and universities and a center for community colleges. In 1992, 52 percent of the national Compact's members were also members of state Compacts. In 1995, that number stood at 74 percent.

Campus Compact was convened initially by Howard R. Swearer, Donald Kennedy, Timothy Healy and Frank Newman (then presidents of Brown University, Stanford University, Georgetown University and the Education Commission of the States, respectively), in response to growing public concern about the moral decline of college students, based largely on the annual student surveys conducted by Alexander Astin. The founding presidents believed that college students would willingly serve their communities if they were given the opportunity, and Campus Compact was founded to support this proposition. Brown University offered logistical, office and staff support to Campus Compact and so its office was established there. In 1994, Campus Compact's membership was 49 percent private colleges and universities: 28 percent public four year universities and colleges; and 23 percent community colleges (all but 8 of the community colleges are public).

Over its ten year history, Campus Compact's agenda for supporting community service in higher education has undergone two major revisions. When Campus Compact was founded in 1985, the primary emphasis was on increasing opportunities for voluntarism by college students, with a guiding vision of helping students develop as active citizens. Toward this end Campus Compact developed technical support for college campuses,

Table 1: Growth in Membership

Year	# of Members
1985	23
1986	113
1989	202
1991	260
1992	305
1993	380
1994	475
1995	517

including Campus Partners in Learning, a $1.1 million mentoring initiative funded by the Carnegie Corporation of New York. The Compact also played a major part in supporting the legislative initiatives that ultimately became the National and Community Service Trust Act of 1990. It was this legislation, growing out of bipartisan efforts initiated in the mid-1980s by legislators such as David Durenberger (R–MN) and Ted Kennedy (D–MA) that established the federal Commission on National and Community Service under President George Bush. This Commission developed a grants program supporting a wide range of youth service initiatives and was the predecessor to the Corporation for National and Community Service created by President Clinton (under the National and Community Service Trust Act of 1993) and then headed by Eli Segal. It is this Corporation which sponsors AmeriCorps, the national service program that links community service to higher education benefits, and that made over $10 million in grants available to higher education service programs in 1994.

The first revision to Campus Compact's direction came in 1989, when Donald Kennedy and David Warren, then presidents of Stanford University and Ohio Wesleyan University and members of Campus Compact's executive committee, commissioned a study of faculty attitudes toward integrating community service into teaching and research. Community service, they reasoned, must be directly linked to the academic mission of higher education if it was to be fully institutionalized. This reasoning was born out by the results of Timothy Stanton's report, *Integrating Public Service with Academic Study: the Faculty Role.*

Stanton's report made three essential points: 1) Expand and strengthen faculty participation by finding ways to recognize, reward and provide strong incentives for involvement.
2) Define a faculty role in which they link students' public service with academic study.
3) Revise the curriculum with the objective of developing in students a sense of social obligation, an understanding of the values of democratic citizenship and the knowledge and skills necessary for effective citizen participation.

Building on Stanton's report (1990), Campus Compact's Project on Integrating Service with Academic Study was created to build community service into the core educational mission of higher education. (See Table 2 for a description of Campus Compact's organizational structure.) Over the past four years this Project has worked intensively with 60 campuses (running the gamut of urban, rural, private and public institutions) and consulted with perhaps 100 more. Compact member campuses who wanted to attend the Summer Institutes submitted a proposal outlining the status of service learning on their campuses and potential action steps for further institutionalizing service within the curriculum. A review panel selected those schools that demonstrated an initial commitment to service learning and could benefit most from the Institutes. The Project's objective throughout has been to help these campuses build community service directly

into their teaching and research agendas. This has meant developing some sophistication in institutional change, especially in the areas of curriculum, faculty development and strategic planning. Most participating campuses report that the number of service learning courses they offer has doubled, usually from ten to twenty courses, in the last three years.

Table 2: Organizational Structure

Education Commission of the States

CAMPUS COMPACT

Project on Integrating Service
with Academic Study*

Invisible College   Regional Institutes
Technical Assistance

(*The Project on Integrating Service with Academic Study is just one of Campus Compact's projects.)

The Project on Integrating Service with Academic Study (SAS) provides training, advice on strategy and technical assistance to colleges and universities that are working to build community service into their teaching and research. While we provide some resources for individual faculty (such as a database of courses and syllabi), we work primarily with campuses attempting to institutionalize service-based teaching and research. Campuses are typically motivated to integrate service into teaching and research by some mixture of concerns regarding citizenship, diversity or building community. Much of our actual work focuses on integrating service with the curriculum, because we recognize that the curriculum is the core institutional structure around which most campuses are organized.

In the most recent revision of its agenda, Campus Compact's executive committee has begun discussing the responsibilities that higher education institutions have to their local communities. Sheldon Hackney, as then president of the University of Pennsylvania, set the stage for this concern in his remarks at a 1991 conference on Universities, Community Schools, School-based Health Facilities and Job Training:

> We have a long-term self-interest in the wholesomeness and quality of life in the neighborhoods around the University and in the vitality, environment and design of the city of which we are a part . . . (Hackney, 1991: 29).

At a 1993 strategic planning meeting, a group of Campus Compact staff and member presidents began talking about higher education's broader commitment to "rebuild community on and off campus" (Morton, 1993: personal notes). It is likely that new program initiatives will reflect institutional concern with rebuilding community, a term that is generally recognized as covering a spectrum that ranges from, in the words of one president, "expanding neighborliness," to, in the words of another, "helping to rebuild local economies."

We recount this brief history because it reflects, to a large extent, the course of community service in higher education over the last ten years; and this brief history suggests some of the tensions that come into play as community service enters higher education. It is important to note that each iteration of Campus Compact's mission has been an addition to the previous commit-

ments of the organization. Voluntarism is valued as well as academically based service; service of limited community impact is valued as well as institutional commitments to long-term community development.

Yet, voluntarism, while it may have intrinsic worth, does not necessarily teach citizenship, nor does it necessarily have a place as an option or requirement in a college course. Service opportunities designed to enliven or reinforce the content of a particular course do not necessarily lead to an improved quality of life in a community. These iterations represent different, if mutually reinforcing, goals. It is important for campuses to be clear about why they are undertaking a project or partnership.

Institutionalizing Service Learning

As this brief history suggests, institutional commitment to service learning is vital over the long run. Eugene Rice, now director of the American Association for Higher Education's project on Faculty Roles and Rewards, has been a seminar leader at three of Campus Compact's national institutes on integrating service with academic study. He argues that, for the integration of service with academic study to be effective, to truly become part of the institutional life of campuses, we must connect service to a "legitimate" and deepening intellectual discourse; and make use of the reward systems currently operating in higher education.

When an academic department or a campus as a whole values service learning, the decision makers will commit funds to ensure its development. They will allocate faculty development funds to introduce faculty to the pedagogy of service learning. They will enable faculty to travel to conferences and workshops to find out how others in the same discipline or on similar types of campuses have implemented service learning. A staff person who can serve as a liaison between faculty and agencies in the community fulfills a critical role for faculty whose time is already stretched thinly.

In order to obtain these resources, a team of faculty and administrators need to serve as a core group committed to service learning and willing to advocate for it. They need to be "organizationally literate" within their campus climate and, at times, entrepreneurial and opportunistic. (The term "organizational literacy," as it is used here, is borrowed from Peter Senge's *The Fifth Discipline*, 1990). Organizational literacy means knowing what is going on at your campus: knowing "how to get things done" through or apart from regular channels, understanding who's who, understanding the normative values of student, faculty and staff, and knowing the history and context relevant to the work you are trying to accomplish. While it's not possible to enumerate what the *sufficient* conditions are for institutionalizing service learning, it is possible to outline the *necessary* conditions.

As Table 3 suggests, an important initial task for the core planning group is demonstrating how service learning aids the campus in achieving its educational mission. Without this link, efforts easily fail. With this link, service learning becomes a vehicle for enhanced teaching and learning, greater student retention and the creation of a true community of scholarly inquiry. Service learning can then gain greater status in the eyes of influential committees. Usually the most powerful committees on any campus are the curriculum committee, the faculty senate, and tenure and promotion committee. In these bodies, the faculty make decisions about curriculum content, graduation requirements, what kinds of research and teaching to reward, and how academic departments relate to the rest of the administration.

Based on the experiences of the five-person teams from 44 campuses that attended Campus Compact's 1991, 1992 and 1993 Summer Institutes on Integrating Service with Academic Study, we have developed a summary list of findings. Each campus was

Table 3: Common Steps to Institutionalizing Service Learning

1. Demonstrate how service learning aids the campus in achieving its mission.

2. Commit funds to ensure development of the service learning initiative.

3. Form core team of faculty and administrators to advocate for service learning. Ideally, some of them would also serve on the curriculum committee, tenure and promotion committee and/or faculty senate.

4. Prepare the core team to be "organizationally literate" about the campus, aware of the history and context relevant to its work.

5. Hire a staff person to serve as a liaison between faculty and community agencies.

6. Allocate faculty development funds to introduce faculty to service learning pedagogy.

7. Enable faculty to travel to find out how others in their discipline and others on similar types of campuses have implemented service learning.

8. Provide release time for faculty to re-design their courses to incorporate service learning.

required to send a team of five people, including faculty members, administrators and community service coordinators, if the school employed such a coordinator. Without such a core team, the Project reasoned, chances of success were greatly reduced. These findings are based upon follow-up workshops with participants, written and phone interviews, site visits and progress reports.

• Campuses are generally adopting one of three strategies, with the first strategy being the most common:

  (1) integrating service into existing academic structure/classes;

  (2) organizing service learning as a discipline or area of study (minors or certificates in community service, for example);

  (3) affiliating service learning with a leadership, citizenship or other "center" that is topical and interdisciplinary in nature.

• Campuses with the most success in achieving their plans are those in which the plan is congruent with a broadly understood and accepted mission, and is articulated in the language of the campus. Those leading the most successful initiatives tend to be somewhat opportunistic in finding ways to institutionalize service learning. This success starts with their own "organizational literacy," the extent to which they know the campus and its competing agendas.

• The least success is achieved where there is not a commonly understood or accepted mission with which to connect, where the plan is inconsistent with the mission, or where the plan is viewed as too "new" or "different." Nearly half of the team leaders remarked that "change is incremental."

• Successful campus service learning initiatives are those in which administrators, faculty and staff recognize the importance of

long-term planning for resource development, including space, staffing and financial resources.

• It is very important that implementation of the plan be perceived as faculty driven. Where implementation is viewed as part of an administration's agenda, resistance is greatly increased and the plan is stalled. This is especially true on campuses in the midst of or just finished with curriculum review processes.

• Presidential and executive level support is a critical, if paradoxical, factor in the success of plans, with these people playing the two key roles of fund-raiser and protector. Often, presidents, vice presidents or deans make critical decisions about the allocation of short-term, soft funds that make or break an initiative. Yet, executive leadership can be counterproductive if faculty and/or students perceive it as too strong or too directive. The ideal situation seems to be that of executive leadership support of faculty initiatives.

• Campuses view faculty course development grants and/or release time as the most important means for motivating faculty to re-work their syllabi.

• Start-up initiatives are very dependent upon the continuity of staff, faculty and/or administrative support. At least one-third of the campuses reported turnover among team leaders, presidents and provosts, and other significant changes in leadership since attending the Summer Institute. Such turnover suggests the need to develop and document institutional memory of the progress of service learning initiatives.

• Those campuses with regular and rich communication among team members following the Summer Institute appear to be having the greatest success. Those with such open communication can most flexibly respond to the changing opportunities and challenges on their campus. Typically, the barriers to communication are the same barriers that stall implementation.

• Typically, campuses refine their rationale for integrating service with academic study as they work through the political and structural problems of implementation. The most common rationale is the relationship of service to citizenship.

• At least one-third of the campuses have doubled the number of courses having a service component since sending a team to the Summer Institute. (An average of 20 courses with service components are offered on each campus.)

We were also curious to know how other issues endemic to higher education affected efforts to integrate service with academic study. While we have yet to draw significant conclusions from the data, we anticipated that turnovers in leadership, fiscal crises or other external factors could influence success. As Table 4 suggests, we found that the campuses participating in the Summer Institutes did experience significant changes in leadership. Addressing these changes often required teams to rethink their plans and expend extra energy, but leadership changes do not seem to have derailed what were otherwise solid plans. We also noted that nearly two-thirds of participating campuses elected to house service learning in academic, rather than student affairs. This decision was of symbolic, as well as practical, importance.

We also found that since their teams attended the Summer Institute, 64 percent of campuses responding to the survey have written support for service learning into the ongoing campus budget, at an average amount of

Table 4: Summer Institute Follow-up Survey Results

After attending the Summer Institute:

a. our team leader(s) has/have

been the same person	changed once	changed more than once	no answer
64%	23%	9%	4%

b. our campus president/provost

has changed	has been the same person	will change soon
18%	73%	9%

c. our campus has experienced other significant changes in leadership

yes	no
36%	64%

d. our campus has experienced other problems significantly affecting its priorities (i.e., state funding cutbacks, lawsuits. . .)

yes	no
41%	59%

e. our service learning initiative is housed in

academic affairs	student affairs	both	no answer
64%	9%	23%	4%

(Note: Out of 44 campuses, 22 responded to this survey.)

$82,100 per year. A full 59 percent of campuses have committed additional staff or faculty time to integrating service with academic study.

The campuses had offered an average of 11 courses that included service *prior* to the institute. Campuses reported having added a service component to an average of 10 more courses *since* attending the Summer Institute.

In addition to the above campus-based lessons, we have also outlined three general lessons for the service learning field as a whole. First, we found that most campuses see evidence of the increasing legitimacy of service learning on their campuses although service learning is still not widely seen as a "serious" pedagogy in tenure and promotion decisions. Faculty believe that a profession-sanctioned forum for faculty presentations and articles, as well as a national organization of faculty who teach service learning courses, would increase service learning's legitimacy. Faculty want discipline-based case studies and service learning conferences to support their efforts in incorporating service learning into their courses.

Second, nearly all respondents expressed strong interest in evaluating the impact of integrating service with academic study. Such evaluation would ideally examine impact on grasp of course content, moral development, perceived relationship of student to larger community and vocational decisions.

Third, campuses are interested in addressing more vigorously the issues and processes of campus/community collaboration. As campuses become more sophisticated about relationship building in their surrounding community, they focus their partnership commitments more selectively, working with fewer agencies in a deeper way.

Success and Failure: Two Examples

It's easiest to imagine the implications of certain practices of institutionalizing service learning when placed in the context of actual cases. The following paragraphs outline two case studies, one an example of a campus successful at integrating service with academic study and one an example of an unsuccessful case.

University A. A large, public institution, had a small volunteer center. It was used mainly by fraternities and sororities whose members sponsored frequent one-time events such as fundraisers for non-profit agencies in the community. Most other students, 50% of whom commuted, rarely used the volunteer center as a resource. The university had a small group of faculty who had experimented with service learning in their courses, but who had not identified each other as engaging in similar efforts. Due to the size of the institution, faculty never had an opportunity to meet others outside their department; there was no annual faculty convocation nor orientation for new faculty. The provost, concerned with the community's perception of the institution as "a research machine" that didn't focus on undergraduate teaching or service to the community, appointed eight faculty members to a task force on excellence in teaching.

The task force identified service learning as one of several approaches that could improve undergraduate teaching on the campus. It enlisted the help of the director of faculty development in creating a series of workshops and brown bag discussions for faculty interested in using service learning in their courses. The small group of faculty who had been engaging in isolated efforts at service learning found each other and formed a core team to promote service learning. The provost named one of them the faculty director of service learning. As such she was given release time to work with the volunteer center and other faculty members to re-design a set of existing courses to include service learning. She capitalized on the Greek organizations' interest in service by targeting the three or four majors most often selected by sorority and fraternity members. One such major was business; students who had previously worked on one-time fundraisers for community agencies now had the opportunity to engage in semester-long marketing and accounting projects for those agencies.

University A started out with few resources for institutionalizing service learning but developed them well by facilitating collaboration. A small volunteer center, a small group of interested faculty, and existing activities of student organizations provided a foundation on which institutional support for service learning was built. A visionary task force leveraged existing faculty development funds to help faculty members re-tool their courses. Knowing that faculty listen to their peers, the provost named a faculty member to direct service learning initiatives but didn't ignore the contributions that the volunteer center had made and could continue to make. University A was well on the road to institutionalizing service learning.

College B. A small, religiously-affiliated liberal arts college, had a thriving volunteer center. Service to others was an important and acknowledged part of the campus mission. A high percentage of students, faculty and staff made individual commitments to volunteer in their community but viewed these activities as separate from their work and life at the college.

A new president came in and announced that he wanted to make the college a model known for its service learning focus. He courted the curriculum committee and, after a year, managed to push the passage of a service learning graduation requirement. The rest of the faculty resented what they perceived as an administration-driven decision that added to their workload without providing any incentives or support. The volunteer

center, which had previously been reasonably successful, was overwhelmed with the increase in students' requests for placement assistance. Nor did the volunteer center have enough staff to train faculty in working with community agencies or to aid students in reflection on their service experiences. Without guidance from faculty or staff, students often settled for placements inappropriate to the college's requirement. Students perceived the service learning requirement as an "easy" block of credits, as hours that had to be completed without the hassle of writing a paper or reporting back in any academically rigorous way.

College B had some of the necessary ingredients for institutionalizing service learning but failed to use them effectively. It had a volunteer center, a mission that emphasized service and a supportive president. But it did nothing to cultivate a broad base of support among faculty; instead the administration, albeit through a select group of faculty, mandated a service learning requirement. Faculty and staff were not even given the institutional support needed to implement the requirement successfully. In the face of these mistakes, faculty and student attitudes soured in relation to service learning.

Although characteristics of each case above are based on composites of real experiences of particular types of campuses, many of the points made are transferable across institution types. The first and most important decision remains: Will your campus ground service in the faculty and the academic experience or not?

Other Significant Resources

Several national initiatives can provide important resources for interested faculty: Campus Compact's Regional Institutes on

Integrating Service with Academic Study, the Invisible College, national organizations and networks, a new service learning journal and a service learning discussion group on the Internet.

• **Regional Institutes on Integrating Service with Academic Study** are offered at seven sites each summer to teams of faculty and administrators. The week-long seminars help teams develop concrete, workable strategic plans for institutionalizing service learning in the particular climate of their campuses.

• **The Invisible College** is an expanding circle of educators who envision and model teaching linked to service and create sustained support for those who share this vision. The Invisible College grows out of the recognized need for an organized faculty voice in the development of higher education's community service agenda. Convened annually by the Compact's Project on Integrating Service with Academic Study, the Invisible College is a nucleus for faculty voice and leadership that promotes the integration of service and learning in higher education. The Invisible College grew from 20 participants in 1994, its first year, to 60 members in 1995.

Educators are invited to participate in the Invisible College by attending an annual spring meeting at the Highlander Research and Education Center in Tennessee. Highlander was selected as the meeting place because of its long history with community organizing and social change. More importantly, Highlander's philosophy is one of "educating to organize." Highlander encourages people to reflect on their own experiences and develop an action agenda from this reflection. This seems congruent with the "action/reflection" cycle of service learning. At the annual meeting the Invisible College,

participants discuss the personal and institutional issues they face in integrating service with learning. Based upon these discussions, they develop an action agenda that is intended to expand institutional support for integrating service with learning.

Twenty faculty selected by a planning committee gathered for the first annual meeting of the Invisible College at Highlander in May, 1994. Identifying their basic mission as faculty development leading to institutional change, the participants committed to three action items: 1) Convene groups of faculty from their own campuses to create a dialogue supporting service learning. 2) Act as convener of a national higher education gathering on service and learning (the first was May, 1995 and the second will be held June, 1996) with faculty and other educators as its main audience. 3) Develop and seek funding for a faculty development plan.

Call Campus Compact at 401-863-1119 to find out more about Regional Institutes on Integrating Service with Academic Study and the Invisible College. To learn more about the Highlander Research and Education Center, call 615-933-3443.

• **The inaugural issue of the Michigan Journal of Community Service Learning (MJCSL)** was published in September 1994. The inaugural issue was funded by a venture grant from the Michigan Campus Compact (with funds received from the Corporation for National Service), and is seen as the next step in developing a publications arm for service learning through the Michigan Compact (following up on the already published *Praxis I* and *Praxis II*, and the soon to be published *Praxis III*). MJCSL was the first service learning journal to be published. The journal is edited by Jeffrey Howard, Director of the Office of Community Service

Learning at the University of Michigan. His intention is that the journal "enhance the perceived scholarliness of service learning as a field." The first issue includes research, pedagogy, and thoughtful explorations of important, controversial and ongoing issues related to service learning. Write to the Office of Community Service Learning Press (OCSL), University of Michigan, 2205 Michigan Union, Ann Arbor, MI 48109 or call 313-763-3548 for more information.

• **Communications for a Sustainable Future and the Peace Studies Association** at the University of Colorado at Boulder have established a service learning discussion group and database that can be accessed through Internet. Faculty, staff, students and administrators can use it to compare course syllabi and program models, discuss implementation strategies and express their views on critical issues in the field. To subscribe, send the message

> "sub sl <your full name>"

to:

> listproc@csf.colorado.edu

• Numerous organizations can serve as resources. Organizations like the National Society for Experiential Education (NSEE) and Campus Outreach Opportunity League (COOL) have been active in the service learning movement for years. NSEE targets the broadest audience and tends most often to attract practitioners in the service learning field. The latter is a national organization of students. In the last year, several other important higher education organizations have started service learning initiatives, ranging from special projects, grant programs and conferences to workshops, committees and publications. The Council of Independent Colleges (CIC), the United Negro College Fund (UNCF), the American Association for Higher Education (AAHE) and the Association of Catholic Colleges and Universities (ACCU) are examples of such organizations.

Conclusion

Clearly, we believe a strong case can be made regarding the educational value of service learning and the need for institutional support. The primary message we wish to convey is that service learning's primary value to higher education is that it improves educational outcomes. If service learning is to gain broader acceptance, further work is needed, however, in "deepening the intellectual discourse" connected with service learning and in researching the impacts of service learning on all the primary stakeholders: students, community and faculty. Service learning would benefit from the ideas percolating in other disciplines, such as the discussion of "caring" taking place in social philosophy and feminist studies, or the implications of chaos theory for social welfare delivery systems. Service learning would benefit, as well, from the practical experiences of educators primarily concerned with teaching values and ethics.

There is also a need for continued study of the impacts of service learning. While the three studies cited on pages 4 and 5 suggest that service learning is an effective pedagogy, they are isolated examples of such research. We are aware of no longitudinal studies at all that explore the impact of service learning on, say, later vocational choices, political participation or charitable giving. Much of the research available is "borrowed" from other fields, and energy is needed for developing more comprehensive "meta-analyses" of the field. It is a historic artifact of federal funding patterns, as well, that many valid research methodologies were developed in the 1970s and shelved by funding cuts before they could be applied. In short, service learning offers scholars from all disciplines rich opportunities for contributing their ideas, teaching and research.

Bibliography

Addams, Jane. *Twenty Years at Hull House*, NY: The Macmillan Co., 1910.

Boss, Judith, "The Effect of Community Service Work on the Moral Development of College Ethics Students," *Journal of Moral Education*, vol. 23, no. 2, 1994.

Cohen, Jeremy and Dennis Kinsey, " 'Doing Good' and Scholarship: A Service Learning Study," *Journalism Educator*, Winter 1994.

Dewey, John. *Democracy and Education*, NY: The Macmillan Co., 1941.

Freire, Paulo, transl. by Myra Bergman Ramos. *Pedagogy of the Oppressed*, NY: Continuum, 1981.

Harkavy, Ira and Lee Benson, "Progressing Beyond the Welfare State," *Universities and Community Schools*, Spring/Summer 1991, vol. 2, no. 1-2.

Hackney, Sheldon, "Papers from the Conference on Universities, Community Schools and School-based Health Facilities and Job Training," *Universities and Community Schools*, Spring/Summer 1991, vol. 2, no. 1-2.

Kolb, David. *Experiential Learning: Experience as the Source of Learning and Development*, Englewood Cliffs, NJ: Prentice Hall, 1984.

Lagemann, Ellen. *Jane Addams on Education*, NY: Teachers College Press, 1985.

Markus, Gregory, Jeffrey P.F. Howard and David C. King, "Integrating Community Service and Classroom Instruction Enhances Learning: Results from an Experiment," *Educational Evaluation and Policy Analysis*, Winter 1993, vol. 15, no. 4.

Senge, Peter. *The Fifth Discipline*. NY: Doubleday/Currency, 1990.

Stanton, Timothy K., *Integrating Public Service with Academic Study: the Faculty Role*, Providence, Rhode Island: Campus Compact, January 1990.

Authors

Keith Morton is assistant professor of American Studies and the associate director of the Feinstein Institute for Public and Community Service at Providence College in Providence, Rhode Island. He was project director of Campus Compact's Project on Integrating Service with Academic Study from 1992-1994.

Marie Troppe is the project associate for the Project on Integrating Service with Academic Study at Campus Compact in Providence, Rhode Island.

Funding

Funding for the work of the Project on Integrating Service with Academic Study described in this article has been provided by the Ford Foundation and an anonymous donor.

From Accreditation to Strategic Planning: An Administrator's Interpretation of Service Learning

Erin Swezey

Founded in 1852, Loyola College is a Catholic liberal arts college which enrolls 3,100 full-time students. Of these, 34% are Maryland residents and 66% are out-of-state residents. This urban Jesuit institution embraces an educational philosophy of developing "men and women for others" through service. Loyola employs 220 full-time faculty, two-thirds in arts and sciences and one-third in the business school. The student/faculty ratio is 14:1. Tuition for the 1995-96 academic year is $14,260.

In 1989 as preparation for its regional ten year accreditation, Loyola College in Baltimore, Maryland developed an institutional strategic plan that revised its mission statement. This new mission, "challenging students to lead and serve in a diverse and changing world," rededicated the College to its recognized history of a strong liberal arts education and a religious tradition of service. The last of seven goals in this five- year plan states that a graduate of Loyola College "will be sensitive to racial and cultural diversity and dedicated to the service of others." As a direct response to this plan and in the same year, Loyola College hired a full-time administrator to establish an infrastructure to promote community service and eventually service learning. This position was funded from existing salary dollars and initially placed within campus ministry, a department which reported to the president.

In the fall of 1991, the president of Loyola College became interested in joining Campus Compact to promote campus-wide involvement in the college's community service effort. He held discussions with the academic provost and the director of community service. As a result of these discussions, the president formed a committee of faculty, administrators, students and service providers from the community to consider how Loyola could integrate service with academic study. The faculty membership represented a wide range of academic disciplines including the humanities, sciences and business. The committee, chaired by a faculty member, was first convened in January, 1992 to develop and submit a service learning proposal to Campus Compact for their service learning institute.

Three institutional events influenced the development of this proposal to enhance service learning at Loyola College. First, the college experienced a groundswell of student involvement in service beginning in 1989. At the end of 1991, annual participant statistics compiled indicated that approximately 50% of the student body had participated in some form of service activity. Second, at the end of the spring semester 1990, the college council, Loyola College's governing body, unanimously approved a proposal to provide academic credit for community service linked to a course through a fourth credit option. (In conjunction with three credit courses, students may add an additional credit similar to an independent study by completing 56 hours of service and integrating their experiences with the course.) This option allows students to reflect upon and analyze their service experiences and to put into practice what they are learning in the classroom. The fourth credit option was first proposed at Loyola College by a Jesuit faculty member who knew of its value and benefit from Georgetown University. For over a year it had been tabled for discussion by the curriculum committee. But given the 1989 Strategic Plan of the College, there was renewed pressure to make a decision about this proposal. It was discussed for several meetings and finally, in a very narrow vote of 5-4, it was passed on to the college council for approval with a dissenting opinion. The third pivotal event occurred during the spring semester of 1991. A pilot program to integrate community service into the curriculum created service components within five elective, core and major courses. These pilot courses provided tangible examples for the potential of service learning at Loyola College as well as small group of credible faculty to lead future endeavors.

During the spring of 1992, the committee met regularly to produce a proposed action plan and developed the following problem statement: "Large numbers of Loyola students are participating in ongoing community service; yet the college lacks structured, ongoing academic contexts for rigorous reflection on those service experiences. While many faculty have expressed interest in providing such contexts, they lack the experience and methods necessary to integrate service into their academic courses." Working from this problem statement, a faculty team attended Campus Compact's 1992 Summer Institute on Integrating Service with Academic Study and drafted a two year action plan for promoting the integration of community service into academic study on campus. This plan was a detailed statement of the college's understanding of the place of community service within its institutional mission as well as a two year, three part plan of practical activities and initiatives to move students and faculty toward a greater integration of service and reflections experiences into the academic and intellectual life of the campus.

The plan, "The Service Learning Initiative," had three objectives:

1. To recruit faculty and students who will explore ways to integrate service into existing courses and departmental efforts.

2. To provide faculty development

opportunities to enhance and support this integration.

3. To assess the student learning outcomes and community benefits of service learning outcomes.

During the first year of implementation the committee focused on the first two objectives. Faculty who attended the Campus Compact Summer Institute and who had piloted some form of service integration with their courses presented the initiative and their initial course development efforts to 40 faculty at the annual fall faculty teaching workshop. Faculty from the committee invited these workshop participants for follow-up, small group lunch meetings to discuss their participation with the initiative and potential service learning course development. Many of the experienced faculty were aware of a related curriculum development, the Humanities Symposium, offering a series of lectures and discussions as well as the common text writing of Martin Luther King, Jr., *The Letter from the Birmingham Jail*. This symposium would be held during the spring semester, allowing time for faculty to develop service components and to connect these experiences with the scheduled symposium enhancing reflection and academic integration. As a result of these efforts in the first year of implementation, faculty developed service components in seven courses. Nine courses offered the fourth credit option.

Critical to this new course development and the progress of the initiative was the administrative support provided by the newly established Center for Values and Service, the infrastructure first envisioned by Loyola College in 1989 and funded in 1992. The Center was established as a free-standing college department no longer directly connected to campus ministry, however, maintaining a collaborative spirit with the ministry effort. The Center reports to the academic provost. The leadership for the Center is shared in a collaborative model of co-directors, one a Jesuit faculty member who sits on the president's cabinet and the other, an administrator, who serves on the provost's deans council. From the beginning, the Center has been funded primarily by the college's operational fund. Other funding includes private and federal grants as well as alumni donations and student fundraising efforts.

Simultaneous to this faculty recruitment effort, a faculty subcommittee of the service learning committee designed a faculty development series offered in the spring semester of 1993. This series included Friday afternoon reflection gatherings entitled, "The Heart of our Community Service" examining the vision and identity of the initiative, a lecture entitled, "Our Faith Doing Justice" given by a faculty member from a neighboring institution known for its service learning program, a faculty development workshop, "Writing in the Service Learning Classroom," and at the end of the semester an off-campus dinner for faculty who had integrated service into their course(s) that particular semester. This end-of-the-semester dinner provided time to evaluate these efforts and to generate pedagogical and logistical ideas and to air concerns for the next academic year. Given the accomplishments and faculty momentum during this first year of implementation, Loyola College submitted a mini-grant proposal to Campus Compact for implementation funds for the second year. The Service Learning Initiative received this funding to support faculty development programs, to establish student service assistant positions that would help faculty with service placements, logistical arrangements, as well as preparation and reflection, and to subsidize part of the expense with the service learning assessment project.

During the second year of implementation, Loyola encountered problems with faculty leadership and limited administrative support from the Center for Values and Service due to sabbaticals and administrative leave. The chair responsibilities for the service learning committee turned over twice, and with each new faculty chair, new visions and approaches emerged. The service learning committee spent many meetings discussing philosophy and pedagogical ideas. Many faculty engaged with the initiative for the past two years felt that Loyola had reached a plateau in the development of service learning. Energies seemed unfocused. Although there still remained individual effort, collective faculty leadership and collaboration seemed lacking.

Other obstacles in year two included faculty skepticism regarding the academic nature of service learning as well as a concern for the politicization of the classroom, an academic advising request for a listing of courses with service learning components to advise students wishing to avoid these courses, and a faculty concern for how service learning endeavors were perceived by the Board on Rank and Tenure. The first obstacle was addressed in year one and two through the faculty teaching workshop and faculty development sessions as well as bringing skeptical faculty into the service learning effort and persuading them of the educational and community value through their own experience. The other two obstacles have only recently been addressed during the third year of implementation.

During implementation year two, three factors seemed to refocus and reshape the initiative. First, external speakers and consultants addressed Loyola's faculty to provide insight and inspiration. In September 1993, Robert Coles, Harvard professor and renowned author, spoke to the college community in a packed chapel seating 800 about his recently published book, *A Call to Service*. He also spoke to groups of students and faculty who were engaged in some way with service learning. In February 1993, a staff member from Campus Compact made a site visit. She met with many of the key players: students, faculty, service providers and administrators. Her report and recommendations spurred us on. With an implementation grant from Campus Compact, we were able to bring a faculty team from Bentley College to work with Loyola faculty, those already involved and those interested, to broaden and deepen our pedagogical thinking as well as ideas for community involvement.

Also during this year, Loyola began its service learning assessment project in earnest. One of the service learning committee members, a psychology professor, designed evaluation tools as well as a focus group process to be used initially with students. Faculty evaluations were also distributed and compiled. At the same time, an administrator from student affairs completed his doctoral research of a comparative study of students engaged in a service learning course and those enrolled in the same course without service. Finally, staff from the Center for Values and Service convened a group of service providers

most involved in our service learning effort to discuss more effective ways of working together and developing relationships with the faculty. This gathering was followed by another lunch meeting inviting both providers and faculty to a dialogue. All of this information, feedback and valuative data helped the faculty, Center for Values and Service and the service learning committee to refocus direction and resources.

During year two, the faculty continued to gather for reflection on their progress and pedagogy. Two significant gatherings contributed to the third factor enabling the initiative to be reshaped and refocused. Early in spring semester 1994, the faculty from the service learning committee hosted a Friday night dinner at the home of a faculty member. This dinner was a pivotal event; it solidified a sense of community among the faculty engaged in service learning, enabled new faculty leadership to emerge and brought forth a serious commitment to service learning as innovative teaching. The dinner also served as an avenue to promote justice both within the curriculum and in the broader Baltimore

---

From Episodic Volunteering to Academic Collaboration: A Community Agency's Participation in Service Learning

As the Director of Volunteer Services at Good Shepherd Center, a private non-profit therapeutic residential treatment facility located in Baltimore County, Maryland, I have come to value the service learning program at Loyola College. Our Center serves eighty teenage girls who are experiencing emotional and behavioral difficulties related to family breakdown, trauma, deprivation, the stresses of adolescence and our changing times.

The Center has a strong commitment to the development of

youth, therefore creating a volunteer program that is inclusive and responsive to the service learning objectives of local colleges and universities. Self-actualization, self-fulfillment, commitment, completion and recognition of accomplishments are key elements in making the collaborations successful for all the partners — residents, staff and volunteers. Volunteer Services incorporates the Center's philosophy which maximizes the dignity of the human person, individuality, human growth

and potential, self-determination, a sense of hope and self-confidence in coping effectively with daily living.

Good Shepherd Center and Loyola College have a long standing relationship that has spanned over twenty years. The Sisters of Good Shepherd who own and operate the Center have welcomed the association with the college and its students because of shared values, philosophy and principles. In 1984, the Center desired to strengthen its work with the college through its then newly created Office of

Volunteer Services. At that time I spoke with college staff about re-establishing a working relationship, providing updated information on volunteer opportunities and participating in the college's annual Community Service Fair.

When the college reorganized and renamed its volunteer office as the Center for Values and Service, the relationship with Good Shepherd was further solidified. In November 1993, when the National Association of Student Personnel Administrators (NASPA) held the first teleconference on service learning, I was invited to be the guest speaker for the audience gathered at Loyola. I have also participated in workshops that have brought together faculty and service providers to discuss student experiences with service learning. Last fall, along with another service provider, two students and one recipient of service, I served on a panel to familiarize students and faculty with the concept of service learning.

• • • • • • • • • • • • •

Some service learning projects developed by Loyola College students and completed at the Good Shepherd Center include:

Three students in an advanced developmental psychology course conducted a series called, "Changing the Channel: Some Steps Toward Better Channels of Communication" with girls in the independent living program.

Students in the course advanced techniques for working with adolescents developed five sessions titled "Unmask Your Own Potential: Discover the Role of Women in History." This series, part of Women's History Month program-

ming, benefited seven girls in one residential unit. The project involved research, biography writing and oral presentations.

Students in an effective writing course involved fifteen girls in recreational activities such as playing volleyball, hosting a Halloween party and conducting a cooking demonstration. The writing course explored themes of individual responsibility for social justice. Students discussed readings on this theme in terms of what they had learned in their service work and in terms of the essays' craftsmanship. Students also wrote on their own views of this topic.

• • • • • • • • • • • • •

At Good Shepherd, the following practices are established for all volunteers, including service learning students:

1. Conduct orientation to Good Shepherd Center: site visit, tour, philosophy, mission and vision of the Center and the volunteer program.

2. Identify student team leader. Usually 4-5 members form the group seeking a service learning opportunity.

a. Team leader serves as contact person for the Volunteer Services director. Performs various duties throughout project duration.

b. Team leader keeps classmates informed and updated.

c. Team leader determines project needs, plans with classmates and maintains ongoing contact with Volunteer Services director.

d. Team leader conducts exit

interview with Volunteer Services director with input from group members.

3. Design, plan and implement service learning project with titles for each project.

a. All members of the group participate. Duration of project is 4-5 sessions.

b. Assess skills, talents, interests and concerns of members keeping in mind the goals of the faculty member for the class.

4. Review and discuss guidelines for work with teenagers at Center.

5. Determine assignment (number of residents, staff support, space, supplies, etc.)

6. Volunteer Services sets up record keeping including fliers which announce each event planned by service learning group. All copies of fliers, confirmation letters and volunteer agreement/program plan are given to team leader and each group member.

7. Discuss sign-in procedures with students.

8. Establish need for communication, feedback, assessment, discussion of concerns, suggestions and review of any feature of the project for everyone's satisfaction and reduction of program break-down.

Avonnee Brown
Director
Volunteer Services
Good Shepherd Center
Baltimore, Maryland

community. From this meeting, the faculty agreed to design and attend a service learning retreat in May to share in more depth pedagogical strategies and curricular ideas.

These factors enabled the service learning committee to redirect its priorities and effort. This year's focus has been on developing faculty leadership, intra- and inter-disciplinary infrastructure, course development and deepening the pedagogy and integration in all service learning courses. To this end many faculty have agreed to coordinate various projects:

1. The design and implementation of an on-going service learning colloquium.

2. The design and coordination of a divisional associates program. (Designating faculty to serve as divisional liaisons in the humanities, social sciences, natural sciences and business as well as discipline-specific consultants for service learning.)

3. The expansion of a college/ community partnership with the Beans and Bread meal program to provide more college resources and expertise to respond to community needs in an adjacent facility and the surrounding neighborhood (e.g., youth programs, economic development, legal assistance, job training). This expansion will provide specific service learning opportunities for graduate courses in education, business, psychology, speech pathology and pastoral counseling.

4. The service learning assessment project determining student, faculty and community outcomes and impact.

These efforts have been funded and supported through Loyola's participation with the consortium of colleges and universities coordinated by the Shriver Center at University of Maryland, Baltimore County. Faculty have received course development grants, administrative support for service projects, student service/teaching assistants and funding for the design and development of service learning curricular and infrastructure projects. Over the past three year's Loyola College has had 33 faculty participate in service learning either through teaching a course with a service learning component or the fourth credit option. The future is bright. As the 1995-96 academic year began, we implemented the service learning colloquium and the faculty associates program. We now offer 21 service learning courses being offered, 14 of these are newly developed courses with service learning components. We have expanded service learning more intentionally in the business school and with graduate courses (of which we currently have three new courses). Learn and Serve monies and existing monies from the business school fund two administrative staff, one to work specifically with arts and science faculty and one to work with the business faculty. One position is a full-time administrator and the other is a graduate assistant.

In a spring 1995 meeting, the service learning committee formed a subcommittee of faculty and students to meet with the academic advising department staff about course listings to address an ongoing concern to list courses with service components in registration publications. Academic advisors also had new concerns about requiring athletes to complete service learning components in courses when they coincide with their season play. This subcommittee met with the college officials involved to determine ways to resolve and address these areas of resistance that kept surfacing. In addition, the committee recommended that the Center for Values and Service, with the input and advice of the committee, design an attractive brochure about service learning and course offerings that would be used as a positive, educational marketing tool to encourage students to enroll in these courses.

The faculty have owned service learning as their initiative. The dean of arts and sciences has appointed a faculty liaison to the Center for Values and Service to provide faculty leadership. Also in May 1995, twenty-five faculty gathered for a day-long retreat to discuss pedagogical ideas and collaborative service learning efforts. Loyola College believes its contribution to the national scene comes from its strong foundation in the humanities. Many of the humanities faculty are involved. Therefore, Loyola plans to publish a handbook on service learning pedagogy from the perspective of the humanities disciplines. To gain this kind of faculty ownership demands perseverance and savvy strategy. Throughout this effort, we have sought diverse representation of faculty from various disciplines to ensure a broad base of support.

Loyola has intentionally invited faculty with skepticism and resistance into the initiative knowing that if they could be persuaded they would become strong champions. Finally, whenever possible, we have invited and encouraged faculty participation in local, regional and national service learning workshops and conferences. Faculty have become service learning spokespersons at board of trustees meetings, college strategic planning meetings and Shriver Center consortium meetings. Many of the faculty involved with service learning view this kind of involvement and leadership as one way to make a significant impact on the institution and for some, it has renewed their commitment to the institution even after receiving tenure and promotion.

As part of the on-going faculty and institutional dialogue about service learning,

the associate provost invited Eugene Rice, director, AAHE Forum on Faculty Roles and Rewards, to address Loyola's faculty at the August, 1995 Faculty Teaching Workshop. The faculty involved with service learning believed that this occasion would provide the opportunity to address tenure and promotion issues. All the faculty involved with service learning have received tenure, so it is the perception of the service learning committee that such involvement does not hinder tenure and in some cases may assist faculty members' service or teaching performance categories. As service learning faculty engage in scholarly and other professional activities, the issue of value and merit may arise. During the time of the initiative, one of the members of the service learning committee served on the board of rank and tenure. This faculty member helps in explaining what service learning is and what its merits are.

Loyola College is once again engaged in strategic planning for accreditation purposes. This time the discussion related to service is how to articulate service learning not only in the mission but as part of the climate of learning at the college. It is a given that service learning is an important part of Loyola's educational endeavor. Today, much discussion occurs around innovative teaching and community partnerships that heretofore was not imagined. Implementation of these service learning initiatives requires time, vision, perseverance and faculty leadership.

Erin Swezey
Co-Director
Center for Values and Service
Loyola College

From Skeptic to Proponent: Faculty Involvement in Service Learning
Ilona McGuiness

I came to service learning as a result of my initial opposition to it. In 1991, I was serving on the curriculum committee at Loyola College when we were asked to consider a proposal for a Fourth Credit Option. This consists of an additional hour of credit which can be appended to any course in the curriculum for fifty-four hours of service work and an extra class project that integrates the knowledge gained from the service experience with concepts and theories learned in the academic course in question. I had serious reservations about this. First of all, I believed all community service should be altruistic. I balked at the idea of offering credit for non-academic work; I chaffed at the notion of putting community service on transcripts. In short, I felt service should retain its status as an important, but extracurricular, activity.

I had pedagogical misgivings also. I worried about quality control. How could a professor monitor, let alone assure, the quality of the off-campus experiences? How easy would it be to resist grading the humanitarian impulse of the endeavor rather than the academic project which was ostensibly its end product? How many times would professors be asked to offer a credit which requires an additional commitment in terms of reading, assessment and conference time? How free would professors feel to say "no," to appear, as we might say these days, "politically incorrect?" And when the discussion of making service a part of the regular course content came up, I became even more nervous. It seemed to me that we had too little time in the course of a semester to accomplish our goals anyway, and now we were going to add extra-curricular activity to the course load. When the time came for the committee to make its decision, I voted "no." My side lost.

This was at the very beginning of the service learning initiative at Loyola, and soon a new service learning committee was established to investigate ways to build a full-fledged program. Our director of community service knew that designing a program that faculty would embrace required taking into account the opposition to it. So, early in 1992 she asked the president of the college to invite me, the most vociferous opponent from the curriculum committee, to sit on the newly formed committee. I have been deeply involved with the service learning initiative ever since. The thrust of my committee work has been and continues to be finding and fostering pedagogically sound ways to integrate service with the course content of disciplines across the curriculum, particularly in the humanities.

In the summer of 1992 I, along with four other members of the service learning committee, attended the Campus Compact Summer Institute. Our group's common goal was to develop an institutional plan for integrating service into Loyola's curriculum. My personal goal was to design a community service component for my freshman composition course. I had decided that if I was going to work on this committee, I had to investigate the implications of service learning in the teaching of my own discipline.

Other things were happening on campus around that time to make me think again about the merits of introducing students to community service within the context of their core courses. Loyola College was in the process of increasing its emphasis on cultural diversity in curricula across the disciplines. As a result, students in my freshman composition course more and more often chose to write on social issues about which they had only second-hand or partial knowledge. I began to wonder whether service learning could help them understand the necessity of "reading" the world around them before attempting to create a piece of public discourse in response to the social and political questions the cultural diversity discussions on campus were raising for them. I hoped that service learning would not only have an ethical impact, but an intellectual impact of a very specific kind: I wanted students to learn that a writer has a responsibility to work from first-hand knowledge whenever possible.

The process of integrating service with my course content led me to become active in a college-wide discussion of how to integrate service with traditional course content across the disciplines, especially in the humanities. I discovered that incorporating community service into an academic curriculum presents complex pedagogical challenges, not the least of which is helping students tie the knowledge gained on service sites to what they learn in the classroom in ways that foster using both kinds of knowledge in the production of academic papers appropriate to the discipline being studied.

The major pedagogical difficulty with service learning is that the experience engages students in dichotomous and sometimes contradictory activities, feeling and thinking.[1] Both are integral to the service learning environment, where personal values are often challenged, tested and shaped. But if service learning is to be an intellectually and academically viable activity, students need to confront, articulate and explain the feelings aroused by the service experience in ways that help them "gain distance and objectivity toward their experience" (Burnham 509). Eventually, students must move beyond the question of values in and of themselves

toward seeing service experiences as sources of data to use in higher level cognitive tasks like "abstracting, summarizing, classifying, categorizing, analyzing, formulating questions and developing problem solving strategies" (Burnham). In other words, students need to move beyond the question of personal values to the academic subject matter at hand, with the self shaping the approach to the question or task they are grappling with rather than being the focus of it.

Like any specialized field, service learning has its own jargon. The term "reflection," which we so often use in our pedagogical discourse, can, when used casually in making writing assignments, prevent the kind of movement described above. "Reflection" is a spiritual term. It invites us to think deeply but not in any particular way. It does not in and of itself cause us, or require us, to focus on one issue. Instead, it invites exploration. Reflection is a stage of thinking where we free associate, where we sort out ideas. It is a stage where connections between disparate ideas or seemingly disparate facts can begin to be made, but it does not imply the necessity of a systematic investigation or discussion or presentation of ideas. The word "reflection" invites us to stay at the emotive level of thought and to focus on the self rather than the subject matter at hand.

Critical thinking, however, denotes a higher order of thinking. It means delving deeper. It means analyzing, and explaining and arguing propositions. It means marshalling evidence to achieve these goals. It means selecting and addressing specific, audiences aside from the self. It means locating the form and language of one's writing within a specific discourse community.

This higher order of thinking can not come before the reflective process, and it does not normally occur simultaneously with it, particularly in academic writing. However, reflective writing, carefully integrated into the course activities, can lead to the kinds of critical analyses necessary to the academic enterprise and, at the same time, give students a safe arena in which to come to terms with the new experiences and new knowledge encountered through their service activities.

A survey of writing assignments given in service learning courses across the curriculum at Loyola College shows that students are often asked to do reflection and critical analysis in the same piece of writing. For example, in a two hundred level philosophy course students were asked to write " a brief (2-3 page) reflection piece on [their] community service project, synthesizing personal experience with the theoretical perspectives presented in the course." Such an assignment gives students mixed signals about what is expected of them. On the one hand it invites reflection, which connotes exploratory, informal writing, and on the other it expects synthesis of two different bodies of material. The latter requires a more rigorous, formal kind of thinking as well as a more formally structured written presentation. In short, this assignment asks students to write two kinds of discourse simultaneously, discourses that require two different levels of cognitive activity and two different levels of language, discourses that have vastly different purposes.

Not surprisingly, a review of the papers written in response to this assignment reveals that students were confused both by the conflicting tasks it prescribed and frustrated by the broad scope of the topic. The papers were often unfocused; students had difficulty limiting themselves to a clear thesis. Most papers responded to the cue to "reflect" and

stayed on the personal, exploratory level, making valiant gestures now and then toward the more formal operations of analysis and synthesis. But the connections between service experiences and course content, when they did occur, were more often than not superficial. The impossibility of the larger task not withstanding, the page-length limit alone precluded a fuller development of ideas.

Professors who make such assignments do so with good intentions. They want to allow students an opportunity to address the affective nature of the service experience, which is an important part of the process of assimilating the knowledge gained through field experience into one's individual, social, intellectual, emotional and ethical constructs. However, it is important not to confuse this process with the final goals of a college course, one of which is learning to produce academic discourse appropriate to the discipline being studied.

Most professors, however, are not trained to create writing assignments which foster the specific kind of cognitive development experiential learning entails. Such training can easily be provided in an informal workshop setting. At Loyola we periodically have cross-curricular discussions of writing in the service learning classroom. There we talk about the distinctions between reflection papers and academic discourse. We study the Lewinian model of experiential learning, which identifies "reflection" as the first stage of a "four stage cycle" in which students learn to use concrete experience in "hypothetico-deductive reasoning."[2] And we talk about ways in which reflective writing can be used to guide students toward this higher kind of reasoning.

Faculty share assignments from the various service learning courses and talk about the kinds of prompts which are constructive, which are counterproductive, and why. We read student papers written in response to these assignments, and talk about their positive and negative qualities as pieces of academic discourse. We talk about how to structure short reflection papers so that students explore connections between the service field experiences and the course content. Students are not required to follow through on each of these connections. Such

exploratory writing however, elicited at strategic points throughout the semester, can help students discover fruitful topics for critical papers, analytical papers, position papers, research papers, case studies and other projects appropriate for traditional college courses.

Double entry journals are suggested as one of several arenas in which students can begin to synthesize the information gathered in the

From Administrative Concepts to Student Realities: One Student's Journey with Service Learning

The student voice is fundamental to the success of any service learning program geared towards the students themselves. It is the administrators and faculty that develop mottos and mission statements to reflect the values the college hopes to instill in the students. Loyola College in Baltimore, Maryland, for example, proclaims "Strong Truths Well Lived," and the Jesuits strive to educate students as "men and women for and with others." Both of these mottos form the foundation for the education that a Loyola student ideally will embrace by graduation, if the values are effectively communicated from administrative concepts to student realities, by way of classes, activities and campus culture. If the mottos take hold, Loyola graduates will enter the work force as leaders with not only practical skills, but also with intact value systems, ready to address the needs of a diverse and challenging world. At Loyola College, one of ways of bringing students into practical contact

with these ideals is through the integration of community service with the academic classroom.

During my first year at college, I enrolled in an introductory sociology class with a service learning requirement. I had dabbled in community service during the earlier months of freshman year, but the service learning requirement gave me incentive to participate in a more intense urban immersion weekend, living above Beans-N-Bread, a meal program in downtown Baltimore. As I later processed my experience of serving meals, meeting people who are homelss, and confronting stereotypes, I began to put service in the context of my classes. On one level, I understood sociology better when I could use the vocabulary of the textbook and lectures to describe my experiences. In fact, I eventually changed my major to sociology, realizing that such an education could give me the background necessary to address the needs of a society with so many complex problems. On

another level, the guidance of my professor challenged me to re-examine my life, my commitments, my values. How can I be aware of such injustices as I have witnessed and not attempt to find solutions? What does it mean to be an active Christian?

My response to service learning, however, was only one of many possible reactions, and it is crucial that the administration and faculty take care to be sensitive to other student reactions as well. Once the plans for realizing a "Jesuit education" are in place, it is only the students who can evaluate whether or not the values are actually taking hold in the student experience. The students have the responsibility, then, of bringing their concerns and successes to the administration, to the very top of the college leadership, even to the president, in order to inform them of whether or not the intended message is actually reaching the students. With any program, there comes a time to evaluate: "Are we meeting our goals? Is this working? Is the message being conveyed effectively or is it getting lost in the translation?"

During the spring semester of 1995, five students who had participated in various aspects of service learning gathered for a luncheon with the newly inaugurated President Rev. Harold Ridley, S.J. The students came from different service experiences, and had widely varying perspectives on what they had done and how they felt about it. A few of the students represented the classic service learning success stories, students whose service experiences had transformed and ignited them, so that they went on to become leaders in other community service programs. Others voiced concerns over "forcing people to volunteer," especially when their schedules already include traditional academic courseloads, athletic practices, extracurricular activities and part-time jobs.

The students at lunch shared their first reactions to service learning, and then gave their final reflections, as they looked back on their experiences. Quite notably, all the students, even those who initially resisted the idea of a service requirement, agreed that service learning is a valuable component to Loyola's education, and should continue. They shared with the president their vision of education: an education left at the classroom door never culminates in real knowledge. To qualify as genuine learners, students must take the lessons out of textbooks and make them applicable to their daily decisions

as students, citizens and friends. Students learn in theology class that Christ calls Christians to love and serve the poor, but can they really contemplate their role in heeding that call until given the opportunity to serve at a meal program themselves? Students study the statistics of poverty and welfare, or the inequalities of education, but do they really understand the impact of these numbers until they meet the individuals affected by these systems?

When the Center for Values and Service invited me to join their staff as student coordinator for service learning, it became part of my job to monitor whether or not these questions are being both asked and answered by the students. In my position, I prepare students for their service experiences, give them information about where they are going, and help them work through their fears and expectations. This preparation work serves two purposes. First, by coordinating the logistics of the experiences, I take much of the burden off the teachers, allowing them to focus more on the pedagogy while I arrange dates and transportation. Second, the personal interaction that I have with the students makes them more apt to speak frankly and constructively with me when they later reflect upon service learning, so that I can then pass on the feedback to the service learning committee responsible for initiating the programs.

In serving as a liaison between the students and the administration, I serve as a student voice,

highlighting the successes as well as the concerns. Along with the other two students on the service learning committee, I offer the student perspective of what programs we most want to participate in, and what programs would probably not meet the needs and interests of the student body at large. As the service learning committee of the college develops new programs, partnerships, and classes, as well as strengthens those already in place, the feedback from my peers plays an active role in the process.

Service learning committee meetings, as well as the meeting of the president and the service learning students created a bridge, the chance for the formulators and the recipients of the visions of education to meet. This meeting planted the seeds for change, for it is only through evaluation that thoughtful revisions can emerge. Service learning is a young concept, still in the process of developing a pedagogy and language appropriate for it. By inviting the students into this process, by asking what strategies are effective and what needs still must be met, students will take ownership and pride in what they themselves have helped to create.

Kristen Ann Cotter
Student Member of Service
Learning Committee
Class of 1996, Loyola College

field with the concepts presented in lectures and course readings. The value of the journal as a safe forum in which to explore the political, emotional, and ethical questions inevitably arise during service work is also discussed. Faculty are introduced to strategies for responding to journals (and other kinds of reflective writing) in ways which facilitate such exploration.

The purpose of the workshop is to encourage faculty to examine both the affective and intellectual goals of the service learning components of their courses. The workshop emphasizes the importance of assigning writing assignments which will help students meet both kinds of goals. Structuring writing tasks which moves students through the developmental stages of the experiential learning process accomplishes two goals: it gives the affective dimension of service learning a legitimate place in the college classroom and it also makes it less likely for this dimension to shape the more academic discourse of a service learning course in inappropriate ways.

Meeting the pedagogical challenges of service learning exacts a toll from faculty. Service learning courses require more time to design and more time to teach than traditional courses. Faculty must decide whether or not they can afford this extra commitment in light of their research, college service and other teaching duties. Moreover, service learning does not fit easily into the constructs of many courses, especially humanities courses, which are not naturally conducive to the kinds of practical application of theory and thought that courses in the natural sciences, social sciences, or even in the business curriculum can more readily accommodate. Experiential learning is more common in these latter disciplines than in the humanities; therefore, significant reorientation is often required on the part of humanities faculty wishing to engage their students in service learning.

To help professors with the logistical and theoretical aspects of such instruction, our service learning committee has recently approved the formation of a network of faculty associates for service learning. This network will begin with the appointment of experienced service learning professors from each discipline across campus who will serve as mentors and resources for new and veteran service learning faculty. These mentors will instigate departmental discussions on the merits of service learning, and they will write papers on the challenges and advantages of conducting service learning courses in their particular disciplines. These papers will be collected in a handbook to service learning. Such a handbook, tailored specifically to the academic goals of our college and addressed to the necessarily different concerns of the individual disciplines across the curriculum, will, we hope, enable more professors to join the service learning endeavor. It is also our hope that the network will demonstrate an organized, visible commitment to Loyola's Jesuit mission to "educate men and women for others" and that, as a result, the teaching of and research on service learning will not only become recognized as important contributions to the ethical and intellectual life of our campus but also be respected and rewarded accordingly.

Ilona M. McGuiness
Associate Professor
Writing and Media Department
Loyola College

Endnotes

1. *Christopher Burnham, in "Crumbling Metaphors: Integrating Heart and Brain Through Structured Journals," CCCC, 43 (1992): 508-513, discusses this dichotomy and the role of journal writing in overcoming it in the process of developing higher order reasoning. He does not, however, discuss service learning or experiential education.*

2. *In David Kolb, Experiential Learning: Experience as the Source of Learning and Development, (New York: Prentice-Hall, 1984) 21-24.*

From Chapel to Classroom:
An Administrator Outlines
Campus Service Learning Progress
Karl Mattson

Gettysburg College is a four-year coeducational college of the liberal arts and sciences founded in 1832 in Gettysburg, Pennsylvania. It is the oldest college associated with the Lutheran Church in America. The college enrolls about 2,000 students (approximately one-half are men and one-half are women), representing nearly 40 states and 35 foreign countries. "The curriculum is structured to impart a broad humanistic vision; intellectual skills; critical, creative and global thinking ability; an understanding of technology; and an appreciation for the interrelatedness of knowledge." The college guarantees breadth through distribution requirements. There is a student/faculty ratio of 12:1 with an average class size of 20-25 students. Ninety-five percent of the 150 full-time faculty have a doctorate or the highest earned degree in their fields. Total expenses are $25,766 for the 1995-96 academic year.

Antecedents

The Gettysburg College Center for Public Service originated in a variety of campus programs, most of which were begun in the college chapel. For as long as people can remember, the chapel had been the center of volunteerism on campus and, as of ten years ago, maintained four regular community service programs: Volunteers for Youth (a local variation of the Big Brother-Big Sister concept), a program in a local development center for exceptional children, tutoring programs in local schools and an Adopt-a-Grandparent program, altogether involving about 125 students on an annual basis.

A second antecedent was a January term service learning program begun by the chaplains in 1979, utilizing the world-wide network of the Lutheran Church for January internship placements for which students received full course credit. This program lasted five years and sometimes involved more than 30 domestic and international placements a year.

A third antecedent goes all the way back to the Vietnam War when a Gettysburg College activist named Stephen Warner was killed in combat and left his GI insurance to the college "to create intellectually controversial programs." In 1983, these funds were used to send a Gettysburg

I am fortunate to be a Gettysburg trustee who has participated in a project with students, faculty and administration designed to expand one's worldview and to encourage the struggle with current issues. Many of the projects present opportunities in local communities, but an increasing number are national and international opportunities. In January 1995 we journeyed to Jamaica and the Dominican Republic under the auspices of the Center for Global Education at Augsburg College in Minnesota. Our group was comprised of eight faculty members, two administrators, and two trustees. We met briefly with a group of students from Gettysburg, Dickinson and Puget Sound in the Blue Mountains of Jamaica where we all stayed with families. The students worked during their two-week stay to improve the community center by leveling the floor. Some of the faculty members who participated in this trip later committed to leading subsequent trips.

Although many students are motivated to participate in service learning in order to serve, the learning component is equally important. The urge to rush in

continued . . .

and provide what appears to be needed help must be tempered by a willingness to step back to listen to another's expression of need. For example, we met with a group of sugar cane workers in rural Dominican Republic. Some of the workers spoke passionately of their need for four-wheel drive vehicles but others, including the local organizer, felt that the timing was not right for acquiring vehicles and that diversification of crops deserved more attention and assistance.

As a college trustee I am concerned with the need to strengthen American higher education; we must all find ways to create an environment in which a student can develop and implement a philosophy of meaning. For me, the trip to Jamaica and the Dominican Republic served as a timely reminder that, while value systems may differ, interpersonal relationships give meaning to life and the inevitable interdependence in our global community requires a sense of responsibility which must translate into public service.

~~ Kristine Hughey
Trustee, Gettysburg College

graduate to Central America to obtain for the campus and the community first-hand knowledge of what was going on there. Others, stimulated by his report, followed, and eventually a sister city program between the Borough of Gettysburg and Leon, Nicaragua, was begun. Since that time from 12 to 20 people each year have visited Nicaragua (we now maintain a staff member there who facilitates small development projects). These visits have done more to educate students about Third World realities in general and Nicaraguan realities in particular, and to stimulate interest in service learning, than any other single program.

A fourth antecedent consisted of several service learning courses that grew up in the department of sociology. One was a January term course on the South, which paid particular attention to the Civil Rights Movement, and which involved service at Tuskegee University. The other, also a January term course, focused on Native American issues, which involved ten days of service on a reservation in the Southwest.

A fifth antecedent was a series of chapel awareness trips of which there were several annually and which always involved service. There was, for example, an annual four-day trip to New York City to explore the response of the Church to critical social issues; this involved service to the homeless. At times, there were also twice-monthly service expeditions to serve the homeless population in Washington, D.C.

The Founding of the Center

When Gordon Haaland became president of the college in 1990, one of his first acts was to appoint a number of task forces to consider educational and institutional innovation. The task force on servant leadership (a choice influenced by the essay, "The Servant as Leader" by Robert K. Greenleaf and coincident with the Biblical concept of leader as servant) recommended the establishment of the Center for Public Service. The president established the Center in December of 1991, appointing the then chaplain of the college, Karl Mattson, as director. Other staff of the Center included Dora Townsend, coordinator of community service, and David Crowner who, with one course release time, continued as director of service learning projects, and Anna Vayda, office administrator.

Central to the development of the Center was participation by a team of five (including the provost and the dean of the college) in the Campus Compact Institute on Integrating Service with Academic Study held at Brown University in the summer of 1992. An action plan with two major goals was devised:

1. To educate and involve the faculty in service learning, increasing the number of courses that have a service learning component.

2. To conform the Center as closely as possible to the real needs of Adams County.

Also of critical importance to the development of the Center have been repeated consultations with many other people and institutions. Our practice has been to copy and adapt whatever seems useful. Of particular importance to us have been: What we learned about the overall work of a Center for Public Service from the staff of the Haas Center at Stanford University; what we learned about the use of student coordinators from the work of Cecil Bradford at James Madison University in Virginia, what we learned about community partnerships from Ira Harkavy and the students at the University of Pennsylvania, and, in addition, we have received much good advice from Ed Zlotkowski and Amy Kenworthy at Bentley College in Massachusetts and from Erin Swezey at Loyola College in Maryland.

In addition, we have benefitted immensely from participation in a variety of educational networks: The college funded the attendance of five coordinators from the Center at the National Society for Experiential Education (NSEE) Conference in San Francisco and the energies generated there continue to run strong; Campus Compact staff have been of great and continual assistance (the Center

has received two grants from Campus Compact, one from the national organization for course development stipends and the other from the state organization funding a regional conference for students on service-learning); staff from the American Association for Higher Education have been of great benefit to the Center; the Aid Association for Lutherans (a Lutheran insurance company) funded a program for faculty on "The Research and Teaching Possibilities of Service;" and the Center is a participant in a Fund for the Improvement of Post-Secondary Education (FIPSE) grant written by Dwight Giles of Vanderbilt University in Tennessee to develop better ways of evaluating service learning, which has resulted in installing such an evaluation instrument in all of Gettysburg College's student testing. Shortly after the Compact's Summer Institute, and as part of the action plan developed there, a consultation was conducted by Tim Stanton from Stanford University and Dwight Giles to assess the climate for service learning at Gettysburg College. Their report both described the situation and set the agenda for the staff:

> . . . we found the climate at Gettysburg for service and service learning to be quite positive . . . we have the sense that the college is on the edge of, or at least has the potential for, significant expansion of service involvement by students and faculty. While there appears to be some wariness now, we detected a strong interest, and curiosity among the faculty. The challenge is to build on this interest, overcome the wariness, and involve both students and faculty in building a service movement on campus, to make the service ethic a large part of the student culture and service learning a significant part of the college's pedagogy.

From Proximity to Neighborliness:
An Administrator Contextualizes the Word "Partnership"

The physical move from the chapel was a significant one for the new image of the Center for Public Service as separate from the chapel. The new location on the campus is more centrally located, more accessible for both students and faculty. There is more space for students to congregate, to "hang out," developing a sense of community based on shared values of service. Separating service from the spiritual element of the chapel programming was also a positive move in terms of recruitment and publicity. Our student population is not a very religious one and many were intimidated and "put off" by the close association of the chapel to community service.

An early and critical decision was made regarding whether the new Center for Public Service would be under the guidance and supervision of the academic provost or the co-curricular dean of student life. Based on the presence of existing loyalties and in an effort to continue broad-based campus support, it was decided that the Center would remain in the student life division. The character and nature of the Center today reflects that initial co-curricular alignment. The service learning curriculum integration which has developed more recently rests on the solid foundation of a campus-wide commitment to service as a part of citizenship and leadership education in a wide variety of student organizations.

In a continuing effort to create meaningful service projects in the community for college students, the Center has developed partnerships with local social service agencies. These partnerships seek to be reciprocal in nature, serving both the college's need to educate students through service and the community's need for service to be done. Despite the social relevancy of a particular issue, not all community social service agencies dealing with that issue can maintain a partnership with the Center for Public Service.

There are a number of criteria which help to determine the success of the partnership. The agency must have an appreciation of the educational process and perceive themselves to be "outside educators." The staff must appreciate the long-term view of advocacy training of the students on a particular topic. There should be sufficient staff with flexibility and expertise to accommodate, orient and supervise the students when they are on site. There should be tolerance of and flexibility with the academic calendar. The personalities and communication patterns must "fit" for both parties. Lastly, the service must have integrity and validity to the community and not necessarily excitement for the student.

The efforts required to maintain the partnership are numerous as well. The ideal is that the staff at the Center demonstrates a willingness to engage in dialogue and offers a sincere and attentive response to problems even if solutions are not easily found. Training workshops for community agency staff and the student program coordinators help them facilitate communication, develop problem solving techniques and collaborate in new programming. Workshops with faculty on "course building" help facilitate the integration of substantial, valid service into the curriculum.

Lastly, the sharing of institutional resources provides an undergirding of strength and commitment to the partnership that exceeds the community presence of student volunteers. The community work study program places 14 students in the social service agencies, providing much needed extra administrative hands at very little expenditure for the agency.

The college computer services has made its expertise available to the community in certain areas. It has developed a strong network with the local Gettysburg school district, enabling the school system to have an advanced, nearly state of the art computer training for students bound for college, vocational training and the job market. Great potential exists to continue to aid the social service partners in developing their computer technology. The sharing of information by visiting faculty or "experts" with community staff, as well as the invitation to community staff to be the "expert" guest lecturer in the classroom encourages a cooperative approach to the role of service learning in education. All these efforts serve to strengthen the ties between the agencies and the college.

The most significant effort to share institutional resources is through the sharing of college facilities with the community.

Numerous events happen on the college campus throughout the year that provide a convenient service opportunity for students and a solution to a social need for the community entity. The Hispanic Fiesta, involving over 1,000 farm workers; Halloween and Christmas parties for migrant children and their families, involving 200 people; parent groups; survivors volunteer training seminar (a 40-hour course); sign language class (a 30 hour course); sports clinics for high-risk children; weekly meetings for at-risk minority high school students; annual fund raising event for the local homeless shelter; holiday party for 180 Head Start preschoolers; and the presence of the Mission of Mercy Mobile Clinic on campus twice a month, offering low-income persons primary health care services are a few of the most visible connections.

Initially the eagerness and enthusiasm for the work caused us all to accept much more than we were physically capable of doing. In our efforts to be responsive, we never said no to a faculty person or to a community request. We essentially spread ourselves much too thin. As we develop more, we obviously grow in our understanding of what the issues are and exactly what our role can be for other entities and within the college community. We have selected three areas of focus within the larger framework of community service. We still will have seven themes out of which the coordinators operate but Hispanic/migrant issues, health and education are beginning to be our prime areas of energy and learning.

Currently at the center of the health focus is the Mission of Mercy Mobile Health Clinic. It is a mobile health clinic that delivers free primary health care services to low-income, "no-income" and the under-insured. The van is staffed with a licensed medical doctor, several nurses and a pharmacist to dispense medicines. Service-related opportunities for students in conjunction with the van include helping the nurses with the intake procedures, translating for the Hispanic patients, helping to care for the children while their parents are in the van with the doctor, and entering data into the computer for the van staff. The educational opportunities are varied and rich. A strong institutional statement of community concern permits the van to be parked on the college campus for the two days of the month that they serve the public. The support services extended to the van include a telephone line for patients to schedule an appointment (staffed by student volunteers), parking facilities, electrical hook-up, a well-lit, heated waiting room for the patients, and access to a copier.

The presence of the van on the campus has stimulated a number of responses from faculty and administrators. The student volunteer positions are filled by college personnel when the students are on vacation.

Additionally, the advisor to the pre-med majors is very cooperative in helping to recruit and advertise the various service options for the health majors. A number of departments have been affected by sharing physical space with the doctors and patients. This proved initially anxiety-producing for them, but, to date, none of their fears have been realized. Several other departments involved in the preliminary discussions of assessing the van presence on campus were the business office, the facilities department, maintenance, human resources, dean of students, and the health services center.

Much of the reaction by faculty to the integration of service into the curriculum has been related to the new information that students bring to the classroom discussion. Some faculty find it interesting and exciting to have the learning outcome include material not in the syllabus; other faculty find it disquieting and unnerving not to have more control over what the course is teaching the students.

Dora Townsend
Coordinator of Community Service
The Center for Public Service
Gettysburg College

Program Foci

The Center has developed three primary foci for its work:

Service Learning Immersion Projects

From its early antecedents in Nicaragua, Arizona and Alabama, now, each year, the Center directs up to 20 service learning immersion projects. This school year there will be 17, one during fall reading days, one during spring break and the remainder in the break between semesters. Most of these projects run from 10 days to two weeks. This year there are three projects on Native American sites, two with institutions dealing with AIDS (New York and San Francisco), one with a major hospital (Crozer-Chester Medical Center), one with the homeless in Washington, D.C., two with the African-American community in the South (Sea Islands and Tuskegee University), one each in Jamaica, Peru, Mexico, Russia, the Dominican Republic, the United States Virgin Islands and Nicaragua. The spring break project is on the Hopi Reservation in Arizona. Participants number about 100 each year. The projects carry an optional half-course credit through Interdepartmental Studies and are led by faculty, administrators and staff members. Credit is given, not for the service per se, but for the learning which takes place. Additional reading and a paper are assigned.

Each of these projects is intended to give deep immersion in realities and with populations the student might not otherwise encounter. According to Cheryl Keen, Sharon Parks and their associates in the book, *Common Fire: Lives of Commitment*, a majority of those whom service providers regarded to be their role models in service began their careers through immersion experiences. The budget of the Center pays the way for one faculty or staff advisor for each trip, believing that it is as important to educate faculty and staff in this regard as students. More education about service learning, its methodology and potentiality, is taught through these trips than in any other way on the Gettysburg campus. Each project also has a student leader who is given a $200 scholarship for his or her work.

The staff at the Center believes it is their responsibility to those returning from such experiences to maintain a stage upon which participants may 'act out' their new perceptions and commitments. The chief concept is that of "sistering", that is, the implementation of projects that stress reciprocity between the service learning site and the local campus and community. In recent years, for example, we have entertained a theater troupe from Nicaragua, a singing group from the Sea Islands and arranged short-term education experiences for Nicaraguan partners. A Headstart teacher exchange was funded by a campus sorority between Gettysburg Headstart and Headstart on the San Carlos Apache Reservation. Each year we bring one or more site leaders to campus for an extended teaching visit. This year we brought leaders from our five Native American tribal partners to campus to improve the immersion projects and to consider establishing a Native American Center. Last year, more than $4,000 was raised on campus for small development projects in Nicaragua. Students host a photo exhibit on campus for area children each year.

In some cases, service learning projects have led to the establishment of service learning courses. There have been three summer study programs in Nicaragua. Two years ago the executive committee of the Gettysburg faculty called to the attention of the staff of the Center a seldom used curricular opportunity, student-originated courses. The students who went to the Sea Islands, upon hearing of this opportunity, organized a course on Gullah culture, for which they received another half-course credit, making a full course out of their Sea Islands experience.

Another closely related outgrowth of this kind of service learning, modeled on an extant program at Stanford University, is the recently begun Summer Community Service Fellowship Program which allows students, in consultation with an on-site agency, to invent a service-learning project anywhere in the world. A small faculty committee decides on the merits of the proposal. This summer, six students received $1,000 awards, all but one of which were for international experiences.

Service in the Local Community

The second focal point of the work of the Center is service learning in the local community. Here, a major effort has focused on developing deep and truly reciprocal partnerships with more than 55 local agencies, 35 of whom are designated as "partner agencies."

A number of techniques and structures have been devised to maintain and develop these partnerships. The most important structure is the way that staff is organized. At present the Center has fourteen student coordinators,

three working with a Learn and Serve America Grant from the Corporation for National Service (designed to create new intersections between the college and a rapidly growing Latino/migrant community), four working with the service learning immersion projects. Each of the remaining seven coordinators function as the contact person with a number of local agencies, which are divided by theme (aging and elderly, environment, migrant issues, health and nutrition, adult education, youth education, housing/hunger/homelessness and volunteers for youth) Each of these coordinators works ten hours a week and receives $1,200 per annum.

In addition to maintaining relationships with local agencies and recruiting volunteers as needed, the community service coordinators have become increasingly involved in 'course building' activity. Many of the newly devised service learning courses in the curriculum require the cooperation of a dozen or more local agencies and these relationships are more often than not the responsibility of students. [1]

Another extremely important part of Gettysburg's emerging orientation

> *As an institution affiliated with the Lutheran Church of America, Gettysburg has enjoyed an historical commitment to service. The college's mission statement reflects themes central to civic education, responsibility and moral development. Service, and particularly service learning of the sort that Gettysburg has established, expects students to critically assess their position in, and responsibility to, their community. It encourages students to meet new people and entertain new and sometimes troubling ideas; it illuminates important connections between scholarly work and the larger society. It was my experience that through linking service and academic study, Gettysburg expected me to gain an appreciation of the limits to my personal interest and recognize the expansion of my responsibilities beyond myself to what and who is "other" than myself. Service learning has become an important defining characteristic of the institution and its programs without abdicating their academic integrity.*
>
> *~Brian Harward, Alumnus, Gettysburg College assistant director of the Filene Center, Wheaton College*

toward service in association with local agencies is GIV (Gettysburg Is Volunteering) Day, run entirely by students from the Center, which involves scheduling almost a full day of freshman orientation for service learning. Again this year, more than one-half of all entering freshman participated in a half-day of service sponsored by more than 35 local agencies. Since each group also has a faculty and staff leader, this meant that more than 400 people from campus were working for community agencies at one time. In the evening, community service agency staff return to campus for a community service fair.

Perhaps the most appreciated part of the Center's community partnership efforts have been the twice yearly Emerging Partnership Workshops which bring students, agency staff, and faculty together to discuss various aspects of service-learning. Recent

---

From Home to Nicaragua: A Trustee Describes the Impact of a Service Learning Immersion Trip

In January of 1994 I joined eleven members of the Gettysburg faculty on a two week service learning trip to Nicaragua and Guatemala. It was my first service learning experience and my first trip to a Third World country. I didn't know what to expect from the trip or the experience.

As a trustee of the college, I am very interested in the learning process. How does a Ph.D. teach an eighteen year old? Can he or she really reach across that gap? From our own experience in attending classes, we know knowledge can be passed from one person to another. Like a Monty Python cartoon, we can open the top of the head and pour in subject matter. This matter can be processed back out and evaluated. We can believe we are measuring learning and call the process successful.

When does lecturing become teaching, teaching become learning, and learning become knowledge? A professor's knowledge commands respect. Passion for a field of study challenges and stimulates minds. Genuine caring for students enriches the classroom atmosphere. And last but not least, a theatrical presentation can electrify this alphabet soup of teaching skills.

But is that all there is? Our dearest wish as educators is to convey this passion, the joy of knowledge, the real love of learning. We wish to teach that learning never ends, that it enriches our lives, supports us in the best and worst of times, mentally challenges us, alerts us to threats and opportunities, opens our eyes to beauty all around us, and can fill our hearts and souls with compassion for our fellow humans. Words aren't enough. We can lecture and we can inspire but experience is the real teacher. It is only when we step outside our own world, get a perspective on who we are, be the odd man out, see the world through others' eyes, that we begin to learn about ourselves and what we think we know. Some writings from my journal illustrate this process:

Jan. 2, 1994

I am ready to go and I don't know what to expect. There are many thoughts and questions in my mind. The people we are going to meet must be dealing with some desperate issues. How do they cope? How can they have hope? For themselves? For their children? For a hundred years from now? Do they think they can make a difference? Why is the college sending a group of faculty members on a trip like this? How does this experience get integrated into academic life? I think this trip will change my perspective on many things; on my CNN-Wall Street view of the world. I'm not very comfortable about this trip and for some reason that is why I am going.

Jan. 3, 1994

We fly over most of Nicaragua which is very green. The plane follows a large winding river over very hilly terrain similar to that of Hawaii. After a small mountain range, the land becomes more and more arid until we reach Managua and two large lakes appear. To the North is a string of five or six volcanoes which rise like cones out of the ground. It looks like a moonscape in the hazy air.

As the plane circles to land, large volcanic craters filled with

workshops have included a number of community agency and faculty reflections on courses just concluded and currently contemplated and a workshop led by Ed Zlotkowski of Bentley College and Katherine Royer from the University of Notre Dame on "The Promise and Problems of Service Learning." Each spring community service coordinators from the Center meet with agency staff, both to introduce new coordinators and to reflect on strengths and weaknesses of the relationship and to plan their program for the coming year.

A good example of the product of this kind of careful partnership building program with local agencies and populations is the Corporation for National Service Learn and Serve America grant received in 1994 by the Center. The concepts and implementation plans for this grant were developed in close consultation with six different local agencies which work with the 3,000 local

---

water appear. This active volcano area had a severe earthquake only last year. The landing is a bit "unusual." The plane accelerates rapidly, pulls up sharply, then descends quickly again to land. As we touch down amid the clapping passengers, a crashed passenger plane lies in pieces to the side of the runway — an eerie greeting.

Warm tropical breezes, palm trees, a small efficient airport and a wild taxi ride into the suburbs follow. There is a smell of wood burning cooking fires everywhere which I later realize is one of the smells of Nicaragua and the explanation for the haze. On every corner, young boys are sellig lottery tickets, cheap telephones and stereos as they walk among the cars. The houses are tin and cardboard, many with front porches turned into small stores. The economist who lectures to us later explains that as a result of the severe economic problems, many people have resorted to selling anything they have or can make. There are no street signs left. Directions are given relative to monuments or statues which are still standing. At breakneck speeds, the driver finds the house where the others are.

<u>Jan. 4, 1994</u>

We visit women's centers, feed-the-children programs, and schools built by remarkable volunteers and farmers trying to pull this fragmented mass of humanity torn by civil war into a new world of literacy, human rights and survival. Over and over I am amazed at their tenacity and their tireless efforts in the last decade. Don't they see their goals are impossible? Don't I see they are not?

We spend a memorable night with a family in the barrio. Paper and tin shacks are homes to these new city dwellers, feudal farmers turned urban squatters. Strangely, there is a softness in the little neighborhood. These warm and gentle people are surrounded by enchanting children who smile and laugh and love to have their pictures taken. They share things they have too little of, extending courtesies so rare for us in our fast-paced electronic world. Our Gettysburg students are staying in this barrio for two weeks.

The next morning we meet with the students in a nearby park to discuss our experiences. They are serious and thoughtful. I am very moved by their maturity and commitment to the people and the work they will do on this visit. A drive through the wealthy area of Managua reveals a small neighborhood, modest by our standards, surrounded by high hurricane fences with electrified barbed wire tops. Windows have massive wrought iron coverings and security cameras. Heavy gates guard the homes. The elite seem to be tenuous prisoners in their homeland.

A year later, my journal still records impressions from the trip:

<u>Jan. 4, 1995</u>

A year ago, I was in Nicaragua. Now I will always want to know more when I travel. The best hotels and restaurants will not be my quest. I am not the same. Images of Nicaragua haunt me. There is unfinished business here, but I do not know what it is. I live in a different space in my world.

Patricia Bacon
Trustee, Gettysburg College

farmworkers, 90% of whom are Mexican. The objective of this grant is to make Gettysburg College, with its people and resources, an important and contributory member of the local community as that community seeks to respond to a myriad of issues and needs related to the farmworker/ Hispanic population. This grant is meant to provide a new and important intersection between the college and the community. The heart of the grant is the creation of at least ten new courses in the curriculum which will have a significant service component in response to farmworker/ Hispanic needs. In addition, a wide variety of symposia, educational events, and celebrations will be developed with the farmworker/Hispanic population.[2] Within this particular context, another example of partnership building occurred when we brought 12 people — three agency staff, two college staff, and seven students — to the Mexican border for a six day service learning experience in an attempt to learn more about the migrant stream that flows into our local county.

At the present time, more than 1,000 students are involved in some form of local community service. In addition to the work of the coordinators described above, there are ten continuing student-initiated service organizations, and innumerable other projects, some brief, others extended. Greek organizations and residence halls are increasingly involved, and the Center is continually engaged in suggesting and facilitating their service projects. This year, for the first time, the Center helped organize a Greek GIV (Gettysburg is Volunteering) Day which will now become part of Greek Week. More than 150 members of Greek organizations participated in sixteen half-day projects.

Curriculum Development

The third focal point for the staff of the Center is assisting in the development of new courses with a service learning component and the addition of service to existing courses. Several small grants have helped us immeasurably to achieve this end. The Aid Association for Lutherans provided funds to run several programs which brought faculty in touch with local agency people and the realities with which these agencies deal. Campus Compact gave us a grant that not only resulted in the creation of ten new service learning courses but facilitated a workshop for these faculty led by Ed Zlotkowski of Bentley that managed to

In my four years at Gettysburg College, I watched the atmosphere of the academic and social communities evolve with the institutionalization of service learning. For the first two years that I was a student, I had only really heard of community service in reference to some philanthropic project that a fraternity or sorority was organizing. By the time I had graduated, however, nearly everyone, Greek or non-Greek, athletes, musicians, administrators, faculty and students of every GPA and major, had participated in at least one of the many forms of service available on campus. Consequently, I saw a change in attitude about the relationship between education, service and society.

I see an evolution occurring in the methodology of learning at Gettysburg College. I believe that both college personnel and students are beginning to see that an education is more than the means to a greater end, that being a diploma and a job. It is a chance to actively learn about that which we are relatively unfamiliar, and there is no better way to learn about the homeless or the poor or the abused than to spend time with them and to learn about their experiences first-hand. Textbooks can't always offer the solutions to today's social problems, but maybe giving students the opportunity to work along with those affected by these issues will achieve a greater end. Gettysburg College is off to a grand start in the educational reform of service learning.

~~ Stacey Zeller
Alumna, Gettysburg College

generate at least three more courses in addition to those funded by the grant.

The provost and the president have provided the Center with significant funds to run other programs designed to educate faculty about the pedagogy of service learning. In January 1994, we brought nine faculty, two administrators, and one trustee on a two-week course to Guatemala and Nicaragua. In 1995 we brought an identical number to Jamaica and the Dominican Republic, which included several days spent with Gettysburg students on a service-learning immersion project in Jamaica. The following is quoted from the publicity material for the seminars:

> The goal of the travel seminar is to experience and evaluate service learning in order to develop a group of key faculty for the next decade in the Center for Public Service. The seminar is based on the concept of service as a bridge over which students and staff travel to places in the world where critical life and death issues shape daily realities. . . You will have special opportunity to accompany various service providers — in areas of sustainable development, health care, community organizing, church assistance, or childhood services — during their work days and experience with them their successes as well as obstacles. . . The style of the seminar is intensive and includes encounters with people and organizations representing many sectors of the countries visited, as well as opportunities for group reflection and analysis. .

The days spent accompanying various service providers have proved to be a particularly helpful way to educate about the pedagogy of service learning. To cite but one example, a young psychology professor, who specializes in children's developmental psychology, in a January faculty trip, had the opportunity to "shadow" street educators working with street children in Guatemala City. She saw the same children plying their trade as pickpockets and prostitutes one moment; then, in another moment, acting out the roles in the extended family they had formed on the streets. Later on, she watched them playing simple childhood games with the street educators, who played such games with them to get them off the glue they incessantly sniffed so that at least for a few moments they might think in a clear-headed way. Not only did this psychology professor experience great empathy for the children, but she saw in these realities opportunities for significant research and teaching.

The other strategy that we have found particularly helpful at the Center for encouraging service in extant or newly devised courses is simply to take time to discover what sort of commitments faculty already have and then support this energy. A physics professor, active all his life in rural electrification, becomes interested in rural electrification in Central America; an environmental studies professor whose field is inter-tidal parasites becomes concerned about the plight of people in Maine who make their living in the tidal area; chemistry professors, interested in the chemical properties of plants, are attracted to natural medicine and the people who practice it. All of these commitments, and many more, provide the energy for the growth of service learning. The strategy is not to introduce new commitments, but build on those already there.

The service component to courses is not, by and large, mentioned in the College catalogue. The Center publishes such information separately.

The Learn and Serve America Grant from the national Corporation has also been particularly useful as an incentive for curriculum development. Up to the present, twelve courses have been developed within the context of this grant.

Faculty and Administration Support

At present, about one-third of the approximately 150 full-time faculty are involved in the programs of the Center in some significant way, forty tenured faculty and nine non-tenured, to be exact. Departments with the highest levels of commitment include: art, chemistry, English, environmental studies, Latin American studies, management, political science, psychology, Spanish and theater.

Gradually, science faculty are becoming involved. The chair of the biology department, believing that service learning would bring new energy into the classroom, has instituted a service learning laboratory in the course entitled, "The Biological Basis of Disease," and has participated in service learning in a freshman course entitled, "Biology and Poverty." It considers the biological manifestations of poverty — malnutrition, disease, unhealthy environments and exploitation by researchers. It also deals with alcohol abuse and fetal alcohol syndrome, dumping of toxic wastes on lands of the poor and the infamous Tuskegee syphilis experiment. The chair of the chemistry department is using his sabbatical, in part, to develop an environmental chemistry course with a service learning component because of his long-standing interest in the pedagogy.

Another chemistry professor, with a deep commitment to and curiosity about natural medicine has added service to local practitioners to her course. Two health science courses, human anatomy and human physiology, require ten hours of service in an agency in which the student can learn about a specific anatomical or physiological topic. An associate professor in biology is developing a service component in the public schools for one of her courses. An assistant professor of environmental studies is participating in the development of a special program with Native Americans that may include a field study component.

From the beginning, the Center has received fine support from the president, the provost, and the dean of the college. The president and the provost have provided the funds necessary for the two January faculty development programs. The Center itself and its role in education for public service is centrally positioned in the long-range strategic plan of Gettysburg and the president frequently mentions this commitment in public pronouncements. The generous funding of the Center is almost entirely a part of the college's annual budget and the president supports this appropriation vigorously. The president has also recently committed himself to raising endowment funds for the programs of the Center.

The provost has been equally supportive, regularly encouraging participation by faculty in the programs of the Center, funding one service learning course with his discretionary funds each semester, providing release time for the director of the service learning projects, and, most importantly, being the Center's consistent advocate. He himself has taught a course on the religions of America. The course included a service learning component related to the Hispanic community. His commitment was developed and deepened by his participation in programs in Mexico and Nicaragua organized by the Augsburg Center for Global Education. His son has participated in two of the Center's service learning immersion projects and his favorable reaction has also increased the provost's commitment.

However, the most important administrator for the advancement and development of the Center has been the dean of the college, to whom the staff of the Center reports. The dean has consistently seen to it that the Center is generously supplied with funds, giving support even to the most experimental programs, and advocated for the Center with all members of the president's council. She encourages her entire staff to participate, lead programs and provide additional administrative support when requested. She is constantly urging us to think strategically about the critical needs of our time and then invent new programs with greater impact. She is not intimidated by failure. When someone needs to prepare an institutional way for a new program, she is quick to do it. Her commitment flows, in part, from participation in a service learning project in Nicaragua. So versed has she become in the issues and the literature of service learning, she has begun to lead consultations at other campuses on the subject.

The admissions office, too, has been instrumental in maintaining impetus for the program. In short, the staff of admissions like information from the Center because it seems to appeal to the kind of students they most like to recruit. Admissions staff frequently serve as leaders in local and immersion projects and are highly informed about the programs. Admissions staff require all tour guides to do some sort of service project and have recently completed a "state of the art" brochure about the Center for Public Service which they distribute widely.

Philosophy

Over time, we have evolved a philosophy which undergirds all the programs described above. A summary of that philosophy is as follows:

Education literally means to lead out into the world. The Center for Public Service exists to lead students and staff out into the world through service toward the goal of increasingly responsible citizenship. It is a major means of contextualizing a Gettysburg College education.

We see service opportunities as bridges out into the world helping students to "cross over" to where the trouble is. There, doing service, the students encounter deep realities at the broad base of society. It is the task of the Center for Public Service to help the student reflect on the social meaning and personal consequence of his/her service encounters. The bridges that service builds are capable of carrying two-way traffic, not only carrying students and staff out "to where the trouble is," but the great energies for change out there in the world (like women struggling for equity, or "walled in" populations struggling for justice) back onto campus as well, turning us increasingly toward social responsibility.

To some extent, we view service as an experiment with one's own identity. Life is always a search for a good self to be. That search is not only the journey within, but a journey outward bound. Part of who we are—perhaps the better part—is a secret awaiting discovery in the needs of those to whom our hearts compel us to respond. Without the man lying by the side of the road, the Good Samaritan was just another fellow traveler. Without the dying and wretched of India, Mother Theresa might have been just an authoritarian nun.

Service also acts as an introduction to the subject of social change. What creates most opportunities for service is inequity in society. Why are there so many street people? Why do we turn 70 or 80 homeless family members away each month from the Gettysburg shelter? How did it come to be that the 15 million Native Americans, here when Columbus came, were reduced to 220,000 frightened people living on the poorest sections of the land they once roamed free? We want students to ask such questions and to search for a humane response to these situations, and eventually to examine the issue of structural change. We want students to understand that much charitable service does more to perpetuate the problems than redress them.

Service often functions as the best way to experience healthy community. (The director or Gettysburg's Health Center often says that the best experience of wellness and health that our students have is found in "doing service.") Communities are sick because of artificial barriers like racism and unequal access to communal resources. Service is a way of bridging, even if momentarily, these barriers so that, at least for a time, students are able to experience healthy community. Service is making connections between artificially separated parts, opening the clogged arteries of society for the free flow of unobstructed energy.

We see service as the best way to teach many subjects. Too much education is standing back dispassionately and unsympathetically, measuring and evaluating and dissecting, as if the student were not somehow intimately related to the subject studied. Indeed, there are those like Parker Palmer and Lee Knefelcamp who see such traditional education as supporting the culture of violence that we all decry. We see service as the antidote, as a way of learning by entering in sympathetically to the populations and problems studied. Like fasting, which although it may not change the life of the hungry, is at least a moment of solidarity with unpredictable consequence.

Alumni

We continue to spend a significant amount of time working to develop alumni participation in the Center. Recently, after consultation with the alumni office, we appointed an alumni advisory board for the Center. In imitation of Stanford, we have created a small organization called Alumns in Public Service which has begun to schedule alumni events that are service learning events as well. Our alumni office is anxious to do as much of this as possible in an attempt to find other alternatives to the alumni cocktail party circuit. (The first two events planned, however, one doing clean up and oyster seeding in the Chesapeake Bay and the other a weekend volunteering in homeless shelters in the DC area, both foundered for lack of registration. But we intend to keep at it!) In cooperation with the alumni office, we surveyed thousands of alumni for their public service commitments and received about 500 responses. These have been categorized and (this time in imitation of Oberlin College in Ohio) we anticipate developing a weekend conference. Central to this will be workshops run by alumni. This will allow for networking between alumni with similar public service experience and commitment and for the education of students as well. The weekend will include entertainment that ties into the focus and a worship service on Sunday built around the theme: the spirituality of service. The board of fellows, the most influential of the alumni organizations, has also undertaken to provide significant funds to endow the Center.

Funding and Staff

Almost all of funding for the Center thus far has come from annual appropriations, something more than $50,000 per year, a figure which includes student salaries. In addition, on average, we receive about $10,000 in small grants each year. Endowment funds are still being gathered and the Center as yet has received nothing from them. At present, the Center has a Corporation for National Service Learn and Serve grant which totals about $70,000 over three years.

The staff is as follows: a director, a community service coordinator (two-thirds time), a director of service learning projects (one course release time), an administrative services assistant, an administrative intern, 14 student program coordinators (each 10 hours per week), a service learning coordinator in the Hispanic community (two course release time) and a course consultant and newspaper editor for the Learn and Serve America Grant (one and one-half course release time equivalent), one volunteer coordinator for the Nicaragua Program, and one volunteer coordinator for center communications.

Karl Mattson
Director
The Center for Public Service
Gettysburg College

Endnotes

1. At every level the Center seeks to involve and develop student leadership. We are aware that unless service learning becomes an on-campus student movement, it does not have much chance to survive over time. In addition to the role played by coordinators (described above), each immersion program has a paid student leader; the immersion programs are supervised by a board, half of whom are students; the large public events sponsored by the Center are conceived and run by students; hiring is done by students. Recently, the Center received funds from the Eisenhower Leadership Program enabling us to hire Dwight Giles from Vanderbilt and Don Tobias from Cornell University in New York to run a series of workshops on leadership and to assist each of our student leaders in developing their own leadership portfolios. In addition, Giles and Tobias will help the students devise methods for passing on knowledge to the next generation of service learning leaders.

2. The beginning of intensive college interaction with the Hispanic/farmworker community has an interesting history. In 1990, the college purchased a large constellation of properties on its southern border with the intention of turning these facilities into student housing. These properties housed a good portion of Gettysburg's settled Hispanic/farmworker population. The consequent communal outcry resulted in an agreement with the college to hire a service learning coordinator for the Hispanic community. This coordinator enlists 15-20 students per semester, each serving as an advocate for one Hispanic family. The student receives, for this effort, a one-half course credit from the Spanish department, since such work requires constant use of Spanish and involves the student in teaching English. This program continues to thrive and has been the catalyst for a myriad of programs providing interaction between the college and the Hispanic/farmworker community. Margarita Elorriaga is the coordinator.